MESSAGES FROM WITHIN

Finding Meaning in Your Life Experiences

Kathleen O'Malley, DC

BALBOA.
PRESS
A DIVISION OF HAY HOUSE

Balboa Press books may be ordered through booksellers or by contacting:

Balboa Press
A Division of Hay House
1663 Liberty Drive
Bloomington, IN 47403
www.balboapress.com
1-(877) 407-4847

Because of the dynamic nature of the Internet, any web addresses or
links contained in this book may have changed since publication and
may no longer be valid. The views expressed in this work are solely those
of the author and do not necessarily reflect the views of the publisher,
and the publisher hereby disclaims any responsibility for them.

The author of this book does not dispense medical advice or prescribe the use
of any technique as a form of treatment for physical, emotional, or medical
problems without the advice of a physician, either directly or indirectly. The
intent of the author is only to offer information of a general nature to help
you in your quest for emotional and spiritual well-being. In the event you use
any of the information in this book for yourself, which is your constitutional
right, the author and the publisher assume no responsibility for your actions.

Any people depicted in stock imagery provided by Thinkstock are models,
and such images are being used for illustrative purposes only.
Certain stock imagery © Thinkstock.

ISBN: 978-1-4525-4449-6 (sc)
ISBN: 978-1-4525-4450-2 (hc)
ISBN: 978-1-4525-4448-9 (e)

Library of Congress Control Number: 2011963148

Printed in the United States of America

Balboa Press rev. date: 02/02/2012

Contents

Dedicated to my mother who allowed me to be in this world and to my children who helped me to experience a richer way of being in this world.

Acknowledgments

My deepest gratitude and thanks to:

God, the Creator and Divine source that has loved me into existence. Thank you for your love and grace. Thank you for not always answering my prayers **exactly** as I prayed them. I love you.

Tom, the best husband a woman could ever imagine having. Thank you for your love, sense of humor and unwavering support. Thank you for being there when I needed you most and for growing with me. I love you.

Reagan, for being one of my greatest teachers. I love you infinity x infinity and beyond.

All of my family for their love and support. Mommy, Daddy, Cindy, Jason and Krystal, I am who I am, in part, because of you. Aunt Starry and Auntie Anita, thank you for being there whenever I needed you. I am also blessed to have so many cousins who have been more like brothers and sisters. I love you all very much.

Jenaire, Trinay, Tisha and Arlene. This is the order you entered my life, but then you never left. Our friendships have passed the test of distance and decades. Thank you for always knowing when to call and for being my other four sisters. I love you.

My spiritual mothers; Irma Gendreau, Bernadette Warwick and Jeanne O'Malley. Each of you was lovingly placed upon my path to guide me. Thank you for your love and encouragement in writing this book. I am so grateful to have you in my life. I love you.

Mark Mariner, my PRH training advisor. Thank you for sharing your "sacred heart" and for your professional insight. I am forever grateful.

God's Girls, the circle of women in my Wednesday night group. Thank you for walking this path of spiritual growth with me. Thank you for your kindness, your love and for sharing your stories. You have helped me to see firsthand how our stories heal, support and inspire. I love you all.

My PRH family; my FRA group, Terre Nouvelle-Canada, Terre Nouvelle-USA and my Friday night growth group. Thank you for sharing your thoughtful insights, for inspiring me, for much laughter and for sharing your hearts with me. I love and appreciate you all.

My dear friends who accompany me in this life. Thank you for allowing me to be there for you and for being there for me. Thank you for adopting me into your families, for your calls and emails and for meeting me for tea or for lunch. Each of you has been a blessing to me. I love you.

My colleagues who inspire me and contribute to the care of my body, mind and spirit. You all have blessed my life in many ways. Much love and gratitude to you.

Balboa Press, for making this a wonderful process and giving form to one of my earliest dreams. God bless you.

Introduction

"I may not have gone where I intended to go, but I
think I have ended up where I intended to be."
—Douglas Adams

I was blessed with a photographic memory. This gift made it easy for me to begin reading at the age of three. I can now see how words were like nourishment to my soul, fueling my desire not only for knowledge, but also for true understanding. From an early age, I was a seeker. I wanted to know how it all began. *Where did I truly come from? What is the meaning of my life?* As I recall, I would get glimpses. But as hard as I tried, my young mind was not able to conceive it fully. I was not yet open to receiving the truths that resided deep within me.

I was a Biology major in my fourth year at Rutgers University when I was first introduced to Chiropractic. Almost instinctively, there was a knowing that this was the path that I was meant to take. Up until that time, my intent was to attend Medical School. I was volunteering at the University of Medicine and Dentistry of New Jersey when I first heard my heart whisper, *"Maybe this is a mistake?"* I would walk into the room of a severely injured patient and my heart would break. I could feel it. I was very sensitive to the pain and suffering of others. In fact, my desire to heal others was born out of pain, although directed by love. I had the *right* grades, but I was not sure if I had the heart. There was also something mystical about being able to help others through the use of my hands. So, I became a Chiropractor at the age of twenty-six.

I left Chiropractic School with not only a degree and a mission of helping others to heal, but also with my future husband. We relocated to his hometown in Massachusetts, were married, opened a Chiropractic Wellness Center, bought a home and had our first daughter. The song for this period of my life was indeed, *"Walking on Sunshine."* I was crystal clear about what I wanted in my life and believed in my amazing power to co-create whatever my heart desired.

This strong belief began in early childhood. I was not raised in a home with religious practices. My parents did not share openly their spiritual beliefs. Yet, I had a deep connection to God. He was a loving presence in my life. Somehow, I came to know that he would answer my prayers. I can recall being on a very small plane at about the age of ten. There were only six passengers. I was traveling with my mom and my younger siblings. There was a couple seated ahead of us. From where I was sitting, I could even see the pilot. We were caught in the middle of a terrible storm. Strong winds seemed to whip our airplane about. The woman began to cry out. I could see the fear in everyone's faces. I too was very afraid. So, I did the only thing I knew to do. I prayed. We landed safely. *Wow,* I thought. *It worked. I got us here.* But, I still remembered to thank God.

There were other tangible answers to prayer which deepened my trust in the goodness of life. I could achieve anything through prayer, I thought. Then one day, life appeared to steer away from my well-crafted plan. My plan was to have two children, but Life had alternate plans. I wrote in an email to a friend on January 18, 2010:

> *I will forever be a mother of nine souls. Four of their hearts, I have heard beating. I have held three of them close and looked upon their faces. And one of them, God has placed within my care, for now.*

"What doesn't kill you will only make you stronger," I have often heard, but never found helpful. I agree that great courage can emerge out of pain and suffering, however, there is a process to becoming stronger. It often requires effort and guidance to stop the spinning, orient yourself, and reach beyond the hurt. At times you have to dig really... really...really deep to find that strength. I am reminded of an adage told to me by a loving woman, one of my teachers, who appeared in the midst of my pain.

> *A man was given a tree to be planted. His first inclination was to give the tree plenty of water. He was told, "No." Give it only a little, so that the roots can go deep in search of water.*

While roots do not necessarily grow towards water, they do in fact grow *where there is water*. Even in unpromising conditions with minimal water supply, they are able to burrow their way through the darkness of the soil, absorbing all that nourishes them. They manage to find their way around and through various obstacles, even changing direction when necessary.

This best describes the current part of my journey. I have traveled through much darkness and I am finding my way through.

My faith, life-giving relationships, my personal growth as a result of re-education and reflective writing were all like a source of "water," allowing me to go deep within to the very depths of my inner being. It is here that I unexpectedly found my answer. It was not a rationalized thought or reliable explanation, but rather a gentle awareness...Each of these lives conceived were all meant to be a part of me and my journey to becoming who I was created to be. I was to be and will always be their mother, no matter the duration of their lives.

I have been broken open to receive the messages that awaited me. *"Amazing Grace"* is now the song my heart sings for now I can clearly see. This book is about how I got to this point. At first, I thought I was writing for other women who had experienced the pain of birth loss and were struggling to find their way to acceptance. Now, I realize that I am writing for anyone who has ever cried out, "Okay God, I'm doing the best I can. What's the message? What am I not getting here?"

Over time, I came to realize that there was so much more that I was meant to be and do with my life. It wasn't just about what I wanted for my life. What I had forgotten is that God had first chosen me—that I was created for a specific purpose and a part of a greater whole. This became clear in a guided group meditation one evening. I write about this revelation in Chapter 10.

This has truly been a journey to a richer way of being in this world. *Amazing Grace* is not just my story. I am not the only being to ever live this. Each and every life on this blessed Earth is a messenger with a gift for the rest of humanity. We are all an expression of Divine love. And, with all of Life's mystery, the answers do lie within.

My intention is that this book enables you to journey within and see the underlying order in your own life. At the end of each chapter, I share messages that have been revealed to me. My prayer is that these messages be a blessing to you and to your loved ones. My hope is that this book inspires you to be **all** that you have been created to be. May you know that God's peace and love has always been and will always be **within** you.

Chapter 1

In the Beginning…

As I approached the final chapters of this book, I was able to better understand my beginning. It became clear that no part of my journey has been without purpose. It then felt important to share the details of my earliest history. That is when this chapter was born.

The circumstances of my own birth were far from ideal. As a result, I was raised by my grandparents on a tiny island in the Caribbean Sea, known as Anguilla. It is an island of fascinating beginnings with many cultural influences. Today, it remains a British territory with queen-appointed representatives.

In the early 1950's, my grandmother left her home in search of work and simply to have a better life. Anguilla, as modest as the lifestyle still is, had been experiencing poor economic times. My grandmother, Beatrice Virginia Harrigan-Hodge, was unmarried and had one young daughter who she left in the care of her mother. It is common throughout the Caribbean for grandparents to assume full-time responsibility of grandchildren, while parents work to provide for the family.

My grandmother traveled by boat to the island of Curacao (pronounced kyur uh sow), and this is where she met my grandfather. The island of Curacao is said to have been discovered by Spanish settlers in the 1400's and was called "Corazon" which is translated in English as the word, "heart." This fiery, adventurous Caribbean woman with beautiful, dark velvet skin was also described as a firm, but loving mother. Together, she and my grandfather had eight additional children. My mother was the second child born to them. She had a brother who was eleven months older. She had a younger brother born in January of one year and twin sisters born in December of that same year.

My grandfather, Joseph McKinley Webster, was a spiritually gifted man with a gentle presence and quiet disposition. I only remember him as a fisherman. I recently learned that in earlier times, he had been a Marshal who was able to calmly mediate challenging situations. People would often respond to his soft, gentle voice. He had also been born on the island of Anguilla, to an Irish father and a Caribbean mother. So, it is fantastically remarkable to learn that he met and fell in love with my grandmother on the island that was once known as *heart*.

While in Curacao, my grandfather worked at an oil refinery. My mom once shared a story of how his multi-race background served him well when there was a racially motivated uprising at the refinery. Many of the workers were injured, but my grandfather had escaped without a single scratch because the Europeans thought he was one of them and the dark-complected people knew he had a Caribbean mother.

My grandparents returned to Anguilla with four children all under the age of four and this is where they lived the duration of their lives. My grandmother, fondly known by many as Mama, was known for her welcoming smile and her hospitality. In addition to caring for her children and mothering many others, she worked the ground, growing much of their own food and also raising various animals, including goats and sheep. She was also known as the "neighborhood doctor." She could find the right blend of bushes and herbs to remedy any illness or pain. Then at night, she sewed and mended garments for other islanders.

My mom would sit at my grandmother's feet and read to her by lamplight as she sewed. At my grandmother's request, my mom would read passages from the Book of Matthew. Just days after my mom shared this, I discovered through a friend's email that it is in Matthew, Chapter 7, verse 7 that reads, "Ask and it will be given to you, seek and you will find; knock and the door will be opened to you"—the spiritual principles that have shaped much of my life.

Most Anguillans completed their schooling by the age of thirteen during this time. My mom left home at the age of sixteen. She found work in cleaning houses on the neighboring island of Saint Martin-Sint Maarten. This very unique island, shared by two nations, is where I was born. Two-thirds of the island is owned by France. The Dutch side is governed by the Netherland Antilles. I was born on the French side.

My mom turned eighteen just two weeks before I was born. No one knew of her pregnancy until she was about nine months along. Shortly after my birth, my grandparents took me into their care. A little over a year later, my mom married a different man who I eventually came to know as my dad. I have never referred to him as a stepdad. He is the only father I have ever known. He did not step in for anyone. Together, they moved to St. Thomas, US Virgin Islands.

My mom made short trips back and forth to see me and returned to Anguilla to give birth to my sister who is two and a half years younger. Then, at the age of four and a half, I was relocated to St. Thomas. I was told that this move was not only difficult for me, but also for my grandparents. While many of my summers were spent back in Anguilla, St. Thomas became my new home.

I always had difficulty with goodbyes, but never thought about how this aspect of my childhood affected me until my own daughter turned four. It was only then that I realized how difficult it must have been for a four and a half year old to be taken away from the only home she knew.

When I first learned of my history, it also disturbed me that I had been separated from my mother shortly after birth. I now see that she made the best possible decision for me. I recognize that I needed to spend my early years with my grandparents. I see their influence in the person I am today, my grandmother's love for the earth and her nurturing ways and my grandfather's gentle presence and desire for peaceful resolutions. There were also lessons I needed to learn from my mom and my dad, so my time with them was equally as important. It is also my rich and varied heritage that helps me to easily embrace the differences in others.

Life's Messages: Take notice of how your world has unfolded. Recognize the significance of your heritage and early relationships. See how key persons have either led you closer to or away from your truest self.

Chapter 2

Expecting a Miracle

Author's Note: If you are grieving a recent loss, feel free at anytime to skip to the Life message at the end of this and any chapter. My intention with this chapter is to show you where I have been, so that you may see how my path has unfolded.

About two years ago, a dear friend introduced me to a book by Robert Lee Camp called "Cards of your Destiny." This fascinating book proposes that my birth card is the Queen of Hearts. It is referred to as the 'Loving Mother' card. It is the card of Mother Teresa, a woman I deeply respect. It also happens to be the birth card of my maternal grandmother who raised nine of her own children and cared for me and many others. So, it would seem that my destiny would be one of loving and nurturing children. Yet, this path has not been seamless.

The following poem captures how I felt in the days after the birth and death of our second daughter. Life seemed to go on for everyone else, but me. My husband found solace in continuing to see patients at our chiropractic wellness center. For me, the world seemed forever changed and I struggled to re-enter it.

A Different Me
The world seems different
at least that's how it appears
or maybe I now see more clearly.

Not only does sunlight seem brighter
but it also feels just a little bit warmer
or maybe I now feel more deeply.

Soft whispers echo louder
and at times, silence seems
deafening
or maybe I now listen more
closely.

The world has changed for me
but not for everyone else.

It seems a bit unfair
or maybe that's just how it's
meant to be.

The world seems different
but maybe it's the same world
and I...
am a much different me.

"It looks like we're going to lose the battle with this one. I'm sorry." Those were the attending obstetrician's exact words. Those were the words that echoed as I spiraled into an unknown world filled with darkness. I was immediately immersed into what seemed like a dense fog. This was June 10, 2006. Our daughter, Jade Morgan, was born prematurely and lived just 1 hour 40 minutes. An ultrasound one week earlier had been normal and there were no apparent concerns. The only "explanation" for our pregnancy loss was spontaneous preterm labor.

That exact moment has replayed in my mind many times. It is a memory that cannot be erased. I remember looking down at my hands and gliding my thumbs along my fingers. I was so numb and needed to know that I could still feel something other than the piercing in my heart. Anything. My tears fell silently. In that moment, I really didn't know what to pray for...or what to hope for. Never before had I felt so powerless. I knew that she had come too soon...too soon to be able to stay.

How could this really be happening? We had conceived even after making the decision to wait a few months before trying again. There had been two early miscarriages within the previous 6 months, one occurring only 6 weeks prior to suspecting this pregnancy. So, this was a much welcomed surprise.

Journal entry dated February 14, 2006...............*Happy Valentine's Day! I'm pregnant again. I admit I'm a little scared given the previous miscarriages. I'm doing my best to let go, have faith and truly believe what is meant to be will be. This has to be the right time. Especially, since we had planned on waiting a few months before trying again. What a wonderful surprise. This is really a blessing...one of life's miracles.*

Seven weeks into this pregnancy, I began experiencing intense morning sickness. I welcomed this as a sign that my body was producing enough hormones to support the pregnancy and that this time everything would be fine. A week later I began to experience light spotting. A visit to my obstetrician's office revealed that my pregnancy hormone levels were still increasing normally. Another week later, I was admitted with moderate bleeding. An ultrasound detected a strong heart beat and determined that I was measuring at about 9 weeks gestation. I was released the following morning after being diagnosed with a subchorionic bleed and told that there was a 50% chance of miscarriage until the end of the first trimester.

After hearing this, I pleaded with God. I said, "If you are going to take this baby from me, please do it now." So when I was well into the second trimester, I was certain that this baby was mine to keep. I was told many times that some women have unexplained bleeding throughout their entire pregnancy and everything is fine.

At times, I wish that I hadn't been so docile. I did not ask if anything could be done. I did not yell. I did not scream. I did not tell them that I believed in miracles, if only they would try to save my baby. The attending obstetrician had explained that they didn't intubate before 24 weeks because the lungs were not developed enough. So, I just had to accept that there was no chance. No hope. Nothing.

Jade's arms and hands moved immediately after birth, but the nurse said it was just a reflex. Each time she listened and heard a heartbeat, I wondered just maybe they would re-consider and try to prolong her life. I was not able to consider the quality of her life. I couldn't imagine what my tomorrow would look like without her. *How was I going tell everyone that my baby had died?* One of my dearest friends was pregnant at the same time. Our due dates were only a month apart. *How would I tell her?*

At first I wasn't sure if I should hold our daughter. I knew I wanted to see her, but I did not know if I could hold her close and then let her go. A wonderful nurse didn't even ask, she just placed her in my arms and said "she is still your daughter." I will forever be grateful to her.

Journal entry dated September 3, 2006....................*My dearest Jade, I held you, but still wonder if I held you long enough. I tried to memorize you, but I'm not sure if I concentrated hard enough. I told you that I loved you, but wonder if you felt my grief more than my love? Should I have prayed for a miracle or did I give up too soon? How could I have not realized I was in labor until it was too late? I didn't know what to pray for, so I didn't. Please forgive me. Please forgive me. I am thankful for the precious time your daddy and I had with you. I am thankful we gave you the name intended for you. I am thankful that we had you baptized. I am thankful that I held you as your daddy leaned over and kissed you. I am thankful that we have a picture of you. I am thankful that we met you even though we had to say good-bye so soon. I will love you always. I will never forget you. When people ask about our children, we will say we've had two beautiful daughters. One was taken too soon, but loved no less.*

Life, Birth, Death
You lived, you were born and
you died
Still your story seems so
incomplete.
My precious Jade, my precious
gem
How could I ever forget?
You are my child today,
tomorrow and forever after.
I am grateful for that brief moment
we met.
Love, Mommy

I did not know that photographs would be taken. My initial thought was that a photo would be a painful reminder, so I chose not to accept any pictures when I first left the hospital. Less than a month later, the memory of her face began to fade. I called to see if I they had kept her pictures, which they had. I didn't want to wait to receive it in the mail, so I drove to the hospital to pick it up as soon as it was available. I appreciated that I could see her face again although it did re-awaken the intensity of the pain.

We held a private service and burial. The arrangements were made by other members of our family. She was buried alongside her great grandmother and a baby cousin who had passed 12 years earlier. I didn't journal on this day, so most of the details escape me. There are only two distinct memories. I recall having a sensation of floating as I made my way through the cemetery. I was not medicated, but felt as though my shadow was present in place of me. The other was a thought…that I had never before seen a casket that small.

In the days that followed, I did take comfort in knowing that so many people held us in their thoughts and prayers. My mom, mother-in-law and an aunt wrote beautiful poems that touched me deeply. Someone wrote in a card that they believed our baby girl was "a little angel in the presence of God." I held on to these words with such might.

Love, Jade
I love you, Mom and Dad so much; I need you both to know.
I wanted to stay with you, but in God's plan, I had to go.
I know that I am in your hearts, your love for me unending.
And here in heaven I can feel
the hugs and kisses you are sending.
We'll always have our moment, when dad

gently kissed my face.
And mom, the love I felt within your arms,
will never ever be replaced.

You'll feel me in a gentle breeze
I'll let you know when I am near.
So don't be sad, I'm happy here,
Where children laugh and love and play.

I'm Reagan's little Angel now.
I'll help to keep her safe from harm.
She'll hear me say "watch out for that."
I'll be her special heart alarm.

There is no pain or sadness here,
the angels all play with me.
We learn to fly on tiny wings
And Jesus holds us on his knee

So raise your eyes and smile each day
And when you smile just know
That every time you think of me,
My tiny wings will grow.
-Jeanne O'Malley

I was not alone in that horrible darkness. This was the first time I had ever seen my husband cry. His world was also spinning like never before. Yet, I felt very alone. I have a memory of him holding me, but I could not feel him. We both expressed how grateful we were for having each other and our then two-year old. Still, our loss threatened to tear us apart. I wanted to remember, while he wanted to forget. It took healing and combined effort for us to find each other again. We didn't realize it at the time, but we each had to heal in our own way.

There had been much anger and guilt in the months that followed. Most of this anger was directed at the obstetrician who had followed me through this pregnancy. Given my prior history, it was recommended that I use an obstetrician rather than a midwife. This seemed logical.

I had seen her the morning of June 9th because I was experiencing some mild cramping and spotting. She assured me that it was a bladder infection even though I wasn't having "typical" symptoms. She said the cramping "was normal" and "could last a few days." She prescribed an antibiotic and said to "drink lots of water." I wanted to ask if she was sure, but I stopped myself. Although, I did not admit it back then, she had told me exactly what I had wanted to hear. *That everything would be fine.*

However, the attending doctor's words continued to echo over and over in my head. His words had implied that maybe if I had been admitted sooner, the outcome could have been different. I was told that I did not have an incompetent cervix or other condition that resulted in quicker than normal cervical changes. So, I had been in labor all day and yet continued to go about my day as usual.

That information prompted a lot of "what ifs." *What if I had gone to the emergency room instead of my obstetrician's office that morning? What if she had done a full exam? What if I had been on bed rest? What if I had trusted my intuition? What if I had prayed more?* For a long time, I wished to redo that day. A few times I actually succeeded in doing so. In my dreams, everything would go as planned and I would have two beautiful daughters. Then, I would wake up and feel the pain of losing her all over again.

Journal entry dated August 1, 2006.........................*I dreamt that Jade was here with us, but then I woke up to find that it was just a dream or maybe I'm just stuck in a nightmare. The tears won't stop. I am overwhelmed with sadness. I don't understand it. I have a loving husband and one beautiful daughter. There are some women who will never experience the joys of being a mother. Why can't that be enough? Am I really expecting too much? Am I just exhausted? ... I miss feeling as though I truly belonged. I feel so alone. How can everyone else forget already? I hope that I can escape these feelings. I'm trying to be stay positive and patient. It's hard. It's really, really hard. I could use a little help right now, God. Please help me!!!!!!*

Being patient was extremely difficult during this time. I truly was thankful, especially for my husband and daughter. It was still very important to understand why this happened. Pre-pregnancy screening tests, an autopsy, placental pathology report and genetic studies offered no medical explanation. There was absolutely nothing I could do to insure that this would never happen again except to let go of my desire to have another child.

Journal entry dated September 15, 2006.................*I know more about health and how the body works than most women. How could I... a health-conscious, deeply spiritual and guided by faith, happy-to-be-pregnant, thirty-two-year-old mother of one...not be able to carry this baby to term? I have provided chiropractic care to many pregnant women. I have known many women who have experienced problems in their pregnancies and still able to carry to term. How could a body that I took such good care of, fail me? This doesn't make sense.*

I like when things make perfect sense. But, I have come to realize that some things never quite add up the way I expect them to. As my daughter once said while bringing her index fingers together, "one and one is eleven." She was only four at the time and continues to change my perspective. She has helped me to see the "dancing leaves" on a windy day, "a chocolate rainbow" after spilling my breakfast shake and "the Eiffel Tower" when you stick a white plastic fork into a square piece of cake.

Today I cried and cried, then felt empty
There was a space that could not be filled.
Then I looked upon my daughter's face
And love filtered in.

Our first daughter had been born at 34 weeks also due to "spontaneous" preterm labor. When my membranes ruptured, she flipped from the head down position she had been in, to a breech position. The emergency C-section that ensued had definitely not been part of our original birth plan. It was not the peaceful childbirth experience we had imagined at our home with our experienced midwife. Since there had been no major complications, we never gave the circumstance of her early arrival much thought after our extended hospital stay was over. We were just so happy she was here, that she was healthy and that we could take her home.

I agreed to many tests, hoping to find an answer for my repeated preterm labor. If there was something to be fixed, then there was a greater chance of a positive outcome. In September 2006, we met a doctor who thought I might benefit from progesterone supplementation during pregnancy. He explained how low progesterone levels could result in early miscarriages and premature births. This seemed like a plausible explanation. I agreed to the progesterone supplementation and to have him follow me closely when we were ready to conceive again. While I had difficulty carrying to term, we had no difficulty conceiving on our own. All I needed was the courage to try again.

Journal entry dated October 11, 2006................*I'm trying to keep my belief that everything happens for a reason. After so many disappointments, it is hard to stay optimistic and have a positive outlook. I'm praying to one day be able carry a healthy baby to term or as close to it as possible. I saw a show on Oprah where a woman's parachute failed while skydiving and she plummeted to the ground at 50mph. She was 2 weeks pregnant. She suffered numerous injuries, underwent surgeries and diagnostic imaging, was given several medications and still managed to give birth to a healthy baby boy. This story reaffirmed my belief that what is meant to be, will be. So, I submit my hopes and dreams to God. I realize what I want is not necessarily what is meant for me. Reaching acceptance has been difficult for me. I ask for the strength, the patience, the energy and the guidance that I need. I am thankful for the blessings I do have. I do have a great life.*

While one doctor had given us the *okay* to try again after 2 normal menstrual cycles, we decided to wait a bit longer. We had seen another well-respected doctor at Mass General in Boston who gave us an NEJM article entitled, *Effect of the Interval between Pregnancies on Perinatal Outcomes, Zhu et al, 1995, volume 340.* It stated that "infants conceived 18 to 23 months after a previous live birth had the lowest risks of adverse perinatal outcomes; shorter or longer interpregnancy intervals were associated with higher risks." Given this information, we decided to give it some more time.

If I could not carry a baby to term or as close to term as possible, I did not ever want to conceive again. This is what I asked for in prayer in the months that followed. Many times I had written *I can't bear the thought of losing another child.* In time, my confidence was restored that I could handle another pregnancy. Again it happened on the first attempt in September 2007. An ultrasound at 8 weeks showed a strong heartbeat and that all was well.

Then, at eleven weeks I started spotting. I was evaluated for a cerclage, but found not to be a candidate as there were no signs of an incompetent cervix. Then at 13 ½ weeks, it happened again. I heard the words, "there is no heartbeat" "the fetus is not viable." Again my world came crashing down. This was only a few weeks before Christmas. What happened? My progesterone levels had been above average throughout the pregnancy. I had been seeing an Acupuncturist prior to and during this pregnancy. Everything seemed to be going well.

I wrote the following entry exactly two weeks before I lost this pregnancy.

Journal entry dated November 23, 2007.................*I had a dream last night that Mama was sitting on my bed holding a baby girl. It scared me a little. I asked, "What are you doing here." I told her she was dead and then she disappeared. I am hoping that this dream holds no meaning. I love you already baby. I want so much for you to enter this world and be a part of our family. It doesn't matter whether you are a boy or a girl... just that you are.*

Chromosomal studies later revealed that it was a baby girl. I now refer to this baby as "Hope" although we never officially named her. I recall how hopeful I had been while carrying her. I had spoken to her and told her how much I loved her. There was already a bond of deep love.

I was asked if I had wanted to see her, but said no. There are times that I do wish I had looked at her. Then other times, I am able to form my own picture of her. Now, I wonder what happened to her body. I imagine her body being shrouded, turned to ashes and returned to the earth. At this moment, I do not know the hospital's protocol at this stage of pregnancy. I never thought of cremation as an option, but often wished I had. It is so hard in that moment to know what to do. I have learned to make peace with my initial thoughts and actions. They are what they are.

I was told there was no physical reason why we could not try again, so there were more attempts and more disappointments.

Journal entry dated April 3, 2008...........................*Today, I am 5 weeks pregnant. I am trying to let go of the fear and not focus on my past pregnancies. It is difficult to do. I have not shared the news with my friends or family. A friend once asked, "How do you get through a pregnancy given what you've been through?" That was prior to this pregnancy. I didn't have an answer right then, but now I have to say, day by day. I pray that each day I could grow stronger in faith and know without question that this will be the one. I know that worrying doesn't help and energy follows thought. I truly want to trust and let go.*

Journal entry dated August 6, 2008.....................*This is my eighth pregnancy and I am again trying to remain hopeful. I want to have unwavering faith and maybe this is the lesson in all this. I have had 2 days of moderate bleeding, but no cramping. It looks as though it is stopping like it did yesterday. This time I hope to give birth to a healthy, happy, 36-40 week baby. I am thankful for this pregnancy. I am hoping for my miracle...The second one in my life. I thank God for the ability to love and be loved. I release my fears...*

Life's Messages: Be gentle with yourself during times of grief. Allow yourself to feel all of your feelings. Let the tears flow, opening your heart and allowing space for love to filter in. Know that you will feel joy again. And, that each day still holds the possibility of a miracle.

Chapter 3

An Ocean of Healing

As a result of growing up in the Caribbean, I am quite familiar with the beauty and limitless nature of the ocean. It is vast and ever changing. It can be as smooth as glass and have an alluring calm. But under that mask of stillness, there is such depth waiting to be explored. Some readily plunge into the deep blue and face whatever lies beneath. Others are gently lured in by the waves that come in slow and steady. As for the rest of us, we get caught in the undertow with no time to prepare for the direction we are taken. There is no escaping the much deeper waters we get thrusted into.

My trust in the goodness of life has kept me afloat during many trying times. Yet, the pain of losing one pregnancy after another really rocked me to the core and admittedly, there were times I was not sure that I would survive. I felt as though I was fighting against a riptide and was exhausted to the point of drowning. So, why couldn't I just stop fighting to have that other child? Why couldn't I just let go of that desire and just be grateful for the one child I did have?

I once heard someone say, "Once you stop fighting for the life you think you are supposed to have and start living the life you want, everything seems to fall into place." I recorded this phrase in my journal. About three years ago, after my sixth pregnancy loss, I came across these words while reading through past journals. I was so distraught this day. As I read these words, my interpretation was that *I should stop trying to have another child.* This is not what I wanted to hear. I tore this page from my journal, crumpled it up and threw it in the trash.

Four days later, while walking the dog I happened to look down to see some familiar writing. When I picked up the soiled paper and saw that it was the same journal page I had thrown away, I saw this as a sign to hold on to it. The trash had been collected three days earlier and this was the same route I took every day to walk the dog. But this day, I was in a different space and these words held a different meaning. Yes, I had been fighting…fighting to carry heavy burdens on my own because I thought I was supposed to.

This was the very day I first met with a woman by the name of Irma. She is the one who started me on a path of healing, growth and re-education. Other than the social worker who came to my hospital room the day following Jade's birth, I had never before sought counseling or any form of professional help. It never appealed to me to join a birth loss group, although I did receive newsletters from Compassionate Friends, a support group for bereaved parents. I was not comfortable with the idea of sharing my innermost thoughts and emotions with others. I had carried much hurt and pain throughout my life on my own. For a long time, it never occurred to me that I would need someone to guide me in my healing.

I was led to Irma at a time that I felt as though I was disoriented, wandering aimlessly and struggling to find my way through. My mother-in-law had taken one of Irma's workshops and encouraged me to see her. I reluctantly agreed.

Irma introduced me to PRH, a School of Adult Development, and the teachings of Andre Rochais. PRH stands for Personnalité et Relations Humaines. This is translated to Personality and Human Relationships.

The PRH approach to personal growth is primarily a journey of self-knowledge and of taking charge of one's life in order to become who one truly is, to know for what purpose one was created, and in order to give meaning to one's life.

-Andre Rochais

This approach appealed to me as I was looking for assurance that my pain was not meaningless. At one of my first group workshops, I was told that *peace and harmony starts with self-knowledge.* I was ready to do whatever was needed to restore peace and harmony in my life. This also resonated with me because when asking "why" seemed futile, other questions started to surface. I began to ask, *who am I, really? Am I truly the person I think I am?* These questions started as whispering, but began to echo so loudly, I could no longer ignore them.

For much of my life, I have followed the rules and made mostly responsible decisions, while being respectful and considerate of others. I guess I thought that pain and suffering would have some regard for this. There was a part of me that wondered if maybe I had done something to deserve this. *Am I truly a "good" person? Or have I been working extra hard at being good as a way to compensate for feelings of inadequacy? What is it that I'm not learning here? Maybe I'm not as patient a person as I thought? Maybe my faith and trust in the goodness of life isn't as deeply rooted as I believed?*

PRH training helped me become more self-aware. It helped me to stop the self-judgment and recognize my powerful inner strength and abundant potential. Workshops like "Who Am I?"

and "Leading My Life" gave me deeper insights about the positive aspects of myself. It became clearer what was solid and steadfast in me and that I was indeed worthy.

I wrote the following on the final day of the *Who am I* workshop; *As I began this workshop, I had a strong will to know myself and openness to my inner reality. Initially, I was anxious about sharing my innermost thoughts and feelings with complete strangers, but was then surprised with the ease in which I was able to do so. With each written exercise, I was able to dig deeper within. I recall in the first weekend session, as I visualized my talents and gifts, I saw them at the bottom of a rocky chasm. Now, it is as though they are effortlessly floating upwards and becoming more tangible. I am determined to progress on this journey of self-growth, now that I have found that inner compass that will lead me to where I need to go. I must allow that compass to guide me as I continue to know my true self, not just how others see me...*

It became apparent that I needed to find what was true for me as opposed to being overly influenced by the thoughts and opinions of others.

I recall a conversation I had with a patient who had experienced two early miscarriages. She shared how she felt as though she was being irresponsible and destroying life by continuing to get pregnant without knowing the reason for her miscarriages. She was determined not to conceive again until she figured out why this was happening. She has since had two additional children. Back then, her words cut like a dagger, plunging me into an intense feeling of bewilderment. *Is this what I was doing? Destroying life?* I also began to question my desire to have another child... whether it was plain stubbornness or based upon a picture of my family that I had neatly composed—a picture that I could not let go of. *Why else would I continue to put myself and my family through such heartache? Why isn't it enough that I had one child? Why can't I just let this go?*

One of the tools of PRH is a method of reflective journal writing. It is when you connect with your innermost self referred to as "the Being;" that non-physical, pivotal center that holds your truest identity, your gifts and your truest purpose. This inner "wellspring" opens you up to others, as well as to a Divine source. This place of richness and inner wisdom can be accessed by locating a felt sensation in the body. *What are you feeling? What are you experiencing?* Whether it is a sharp pain, mild discomfort, positive or negative feeling, intense emotion, subtle uneasiness or tinge of excitement, you pay specific attention to whatever is felt, physically or psychologically. You trust that this sensation is signaling something meaningful. Then, you write whatever this process awakens in you. You explore, describing all that surrounds this sensation, breaking it apart until you are led deeper and deeper. You enter the inner depths of yourself with the intention of discovering or experiencing something new—a new aspect of yourself, more clarity, a freeing, anything that allows you to live your life better.

As I took the time to get in touch with my deepest self, I began to see things in a much different light. I realized that my desire to have a second child came from an inner knowing that there was to be another child in my life. In that very moment, I had a recollection of a time when I had felt the exact way. It was when I was very young. I had unexplainable thoughts that I was supposed to have a second sister. At that time, I had one sister who was two and a half years younger and our brother was two years younger than she was. I could not figure out why I was having these feelings. One day, I asked my mom if I had another sister who died. When she said, "no," I don't recall whether or not I ever thought of this again. Even thirteen years later when my second sister was born, I can't remember if those earlier thoughts ever re-entered my mind. As I wrote the following entry, this memory flooded my mind and those feelings re-surfaced.

Growth Journal entry dated January 13, 2009....................... *I have searched for the answers to my pregnancy losses, but they are none. There is nothing to be fixed. No treatment to undergo. It is not my intent to destroy a life, but rather to create a life I feel is supposed to be. I have that sense. It's really hard to explain. It's as though there is a memory that seems so alive I can almost see it, but no matter how far into the memory bank I go, I can't seem to get a clear enough picture of it. It's like when I felt that I was to have another sister. That's exactly it. I remember asking my mom if I had another sister who died. I didn't understand it then. But now I do. It wasn't just a dream I had. It was something I caught a glimpse of and felt within.*

I have come to trust the process of exploring my sensations. What seems illogical at first can lead to much clarity. When certain unexplained thoughts or memories arise at a specific moment, I no longer shun them or view them as mere sentiments or functions of my imagination. My analytical nature caused me to ignore many insights in the past. *That couldn't be,* I would tell myself. It took much awareness to learn to trust in that deepest part of me.

During times of grief, past memories and feelings have surfaced quite readily and with such unexpected intensity. It was as though my present tears were awakening those that I cried a long time ago. Past hurts seemed utterly fresh and dormant wounds began to open. The use of a growth journal allowed me to better understand these feelings and know exactly what I was living. As Irma says, "A sensation has something to teach us and writing deepens the experience, helping you to experience it to the fullest."

Growth Journal entry dated May 18, 2010....................*As I bring my awareness to my deepest self, I ask, "What is most alive in me?" The sensation of sadness is very much alive. I have so much to be grateful for. I want to remain in the state of gratitude. But at this very moment, there is heaviness in my chest and it aches. I cannot deny this. I am sad because of all the loss my family has endured. I am sad because no matter my efforts, I have not been able to carry a child to term. The tears keep flowing. I just want this hurt to stop! It is too great and feels like its awakening even more pain. The pain of having my innocence stripped away as a child feels like its being ignited. Why am I rocking back and forth? I thought I had made peace with this. Why is this still coming up? Thoughts of my mom being violated at the age of 17 enter my mind. It still hurts knowing that I was conceived this way. I also think about my bond with her being broken when my grandparents took me into their care as an infant. They didn't think she could take care of me. Then when I think of being four and a half and having to say goodbye to my grandparents....... (The quiet tears became uncontrollable sobs)..... Okay. Breathe. I'm glad to know my mom did not abandon me; still, I can't help but cry for the young child who was taken away from the only home she knew...... I understand it now. It is not just the pain of today or recent times. It's all the pain and loss that has existed throughout my life that is linked to this sadness I feel today. While I survived and overcame much, there is still an ocean to unmask in order to reclaim the parts of me that were lost along the way. Yes, I want to be whole. I see how my growth is opening me up to healing. I need to be gentle with myself. I can't heal everything in a day or even a few years. Geez, this could even take a lifetime. I honestly don't think I realized that until this very moment.*

This form of reflective journal writing has been an important means for my growth and healing. It has allowed me to decipher a density of emotions and given me a clearer sense of who I am and what is essential in me. It has helped me to see my feelings of self-doubt as symptoms of past humiliations and criticisms that were left behind. It has taken much effort and support to affirm that I am more than adequate and that I deserve the same level of respect that I so willingly give to others. I have gotten better at facing criticisms; not because I grew "thicker skin," but by learning to let go of others' opinions without losing myself to them. I have been able to regain trust in the workings of my body, trust in my intuition, trust in the fact that I was meant to be in this world and trust in the intricacy of this world that surrounds me. I recognize that I do not have to be flawless; I just have to be me.

Simply Perfect
Who says you're not perfect?

Is it not perfection that you were created out of nothingness or rather, greatness; that though we take note of our outward differences, within, we are physically the same?

Is it not perfect that it takes two distinct beings, man and woman, to create another perfect being?

That a baby, weighing only a pound can still grow, can still learn and can still become all that she is meant to be?

Is it not perfect that a cut heals without much attention? That you breathe without much effort?

Is it not perfect that you can feel joyous, satisfied, inspired, loved?
That you can cry when you need to, but that the tears don't last forever

Is it not perfect that love can heal?

Who says there is no such thing as perfection?
I am perfectly me and you are perfectly you.
Now is that not...simply perfect.

There was a time when I thought that complete healing was a goal. I now understand that it is an ongoing process that I could not have ordered at will. My inner being aspires to exist fully and live abundantly. My deepest self wants me to continue on this path of growth and healing, being present to each part of the journey, trusting that I am being guided and I will end up exactly where I am meant to be.

Life's Messages: Healing from the past is about reclaiming the essential parts of who you are in order to live more fully in the present. Recognize that you need others to facilitate your growth and healing. Connect with you innermost self to identify your greatness and to better understand your life experiences.

Chapter 4

By Thy Grace

A New Year's Prayer

May God make your year a happy one!
Not by shielding you from all sorrows and pain,
But by strengthening you to bear it, as it comes;
Not by making your path easy,
But by making you sturdy to travel any path.
Not by taking hardships from you,
But by taking fear from your heart;
Not by granting you unbroken sunshine,
But by keeping your face bright, even in the shadows;
Not by making your life always pleasant,
But by showing you when people and their causes need
you most,
And by making you anxious to be there to help.
God's love, peace, hope and joy to you for the year
ahead.
Author Unknown

There is often much reflection and hope when we usher in a new
year. It is not only a time of great celebration, but also viewed by

many as "a new beginning." It is one of the few times we make promises to ourselves and to no one else. We are motivated to want new things, change our lifestyles, and have more meaningful experiences. We resolve to get it right this time…to do better than we have in previous years.

For me, this was going to be the year I would successfully give birth to another child. We had agreed that this would be our final attempt. This time, we had tried and done everything that we thought possible. I had been on strict bed rest for four weeks, with only bathroom privileges. I had received weekly progesterone injections to help prevent another pre-term labor. I had continued to take exceptional care of my body and visualize holding a healthy, happy baby boy in my arms. How could this not be enough?

About one o'clock in the afternoon on New Year's Eve I was admitted for the second time in this pregnancy. Gushing, but clear fluids signaled impending preterm labor. A strong heartbeat and good movement offered hope. A wonderful nurse reminded me that "miracles happen" and that it was not impossible for ruptured membranes to seal over. A wise friend and teacher reminded me that I did not have to live it before it happened. I had resolved to keep hoping for the best. I continued to pray that our son would be okay.

I prayed with all my heart just as I had done the night before in my dream. In this dream, I was in a huge crowd and somehow got separated from my daughter. I was in such a panic because I could not find her anywhere. I was aware of this current pregnancy. I prayed with all my might and told God that I would give anything to see my daughter again, but I did not want to choose between her and this new baby.

As hard as I prayed, I also cried. I cried because I was afraid. I was afraid that our son would not survive. I was afraid that our marriage would not survive another loss. I was afraid that our daughter who very much looking forward to having a brother, would be heart-broken. I was afraid that many of our family and friends would think that their prayers went unanswered. I was afraid of all that could happen.

December 31, 2009...*I am in the hospital this New Year's Eve. What am I feeling? I am scared. Why couldn't this pregnancy be just a little bit easier than the others? It's been a long road. It is not the way I imagined ringing in 2010. I am still hopeful, though. There is no pain. My baby boy is still alive and kicking. All is well in this very moment. The nurse just checked his heartbeat again. It was really good to hear such a beautiful sound. In fact, I can still hear it echoing in my head. I love you so much, my sweet baby. All along I have been praying for you to be born healthy, but I will accept you however God wants to give you to me. I will love you no matter what. If you can stay in there just a few more weeks, we'll have a better chance. I know it won't be easy, but I am not ready to say goodbye to you. We can do this...Tomorrow is a brand new year, a new decade. I guess my only resolution is to take it one moment at a time.*

It requires much practice to remain in the present and not live a painful event before it actually occurs. How do you remain hopeful when others say otherwise? I was asked repeatedly if I had wanted to be induced. I declined each time. If there was a remote possibility that I could carry this baby just a few more weeks, I wanted that chance, even though I knew he would be at risk for numerous health challenges. For the first time, it occurred to me that no one ever prays for a differently-abled child or a child requiring special needs. Yes, I wanted a healthy child, but I was willing to accept this baby however God intended him to be. How could I agree to the induction knowing that there was still a heartbeat? I just could not make that decision.

By mid-afternoon on New Year's Day, I knew that labor was imminent. My husband was scheduled to perform in Rhode Island with his cover band and I decided not to tell him that I sensed I was in labor. This was not to shield him from another painful loss. Yes, I wanted him to see our son. Yes, I knew he would want to see me through this. At the same time, I would have been more focused on his feelings rather than my own. I knew that this would be my last opportunity to give birth. I wanted this to be my main focus in spite of the outcome.

I called a trusted friend to be with me so that I would have additional support. I asked that my husband not be called until absolutely necessary. I progressed into labor without any augmentation later that evening. I delivered our baby at 11:10 pm. He was stillborn. This time I knew without question that I wanted to see my baby and hold him. I did so, but only briefly at that time because of post-delivery complications.

I had retained the placenta and was taken to the operating room for a D&C. I began to bleed briskly and suddenly felt weak and light-headed. Spinal anesthesia was attempted, but unsuccessful. My obstetrician who had been in the hospital delivering another patient joined the team in the operating room. She made her presence known to me. It was comforting to see a familiar face under these circumstances. I heard her say to the anesthesiologist, "we need to move to general anesthetic." I had to undergo general anesthesia which was once a tremendous fear of mine.

In a prior D&C in December 2007, I was told that general anesthesia would be used. At that particular time, I reluctantly agreed. But, for whatever reason the anesthesiologist changed his mind once we were in the operating room and decided to perform spinal anesthesia. I often wondered if he saw the fear in my eyes. It was the fear of giving up complete control of my body.

This time, there was no time to consider the fact that I would be completely unaware of what would be done to me. I was aware that I had suffered significant blood loss and heard someone say with much urgency, "we need to get some fluids into her." My final words before the anesthesia completely took effect were, "I can't breathe." My last thoughts were *God, I know it's going to be hard living with another loss, but I need to be here for my daughter.*

By the grace of God, I awoke fully about ten or eleven hours later in the surgical intensive care unit. My first reaction was panic when I realized that I had been intubated. I recall the respiratory therapist's words, "You're okay, just try to breathe with the machine." I was told that my lungs would have to be checked before the tubes could be removed. So, I would have to wait for the attending doctor. This seemed endless. All I could think was *after everything else, how could this be happening?*

The reason for the breathing tubes was hemodynamic instability. I had lost more than half of my blood volume and there had been inadequate blood flow which was life-threatening. I was told that I had received a series of transfusions and that I would be "okay."

I remember being asked during a prenatal visit if I consent to receiving a blood transfusion if it was ever necessary. With much hesitation, I had stated, "I have to consider my daughter, so I guess I would." At that time, the idea of being transfused with another person's blood was scary to me, but seemed highly unlikely. I never imagined that it would ever be a reality.

I later learned that many maneuvers had been attempted before the bleeding stopped. My husband had arrived while I was in the operating room and was told that I did receive blood although no formal consents were signed because it was a life or death situation. He was also told that I would be getting other blood products and that a hysterectomy may be necessary if the bleeding continued. He was agreeable to all this.

He had not been allowed to stay at my bedside while I was sedated. One of my nurses explained that each time he came into the room my heart rate accelerated. I have no recollection of this, but I do recall seeing him standing out in the hall as I was first waking. As I became fully conscious, he was allowed in. He held my hand while we waited for the breathing tubes to be removed. One of the first things I asked was if he saw our son. He just nodded and bent over to hug me.

Our son, Jackson Thomas, was baptized on the 2nd of January. This was for me rather than for him. I do not believe that he was born with "original sin." It was more of a ritual, so that I could have another memory of him. That is what I needed during this time.

Jackson was buried alongside his sister, Jade, on January 9, 2010. I understood the importance of these in rituals in our healing, but it was still such a sad day. We had decided not to invite family or friends to the graveside service. I began this day in prayer, asking God to be with my husband, daughter and I as we said goodbye. That morning, I was also drawn to Doreen Virtue's archangel oracle cards and recorded two of the cards that I drew.

The first was Comfort, Archangel Azrael: "I am with you in your time of need, helping your heart to heal." The second card was Teaching and Learning, Archangel Zadkiel: "Keep an open mind and learn new ideas. Then, teach these ideas to others." The relevance of the second became evident as time passed, which I will explain later. These cards were clear signs of grace during this critical time.

Grace was also present when we told our five-year-old daughter that her brother had died. Before leaving the hospital, I had spoken with a social worker about how to approach this given her young age. She advised that we be honest and phrase our responses so that we were only answering the questions that were asked. We were not to give any information that she didn't ask for. Still, I wasn't sure how to even begin this dreaded conversation.

She had been only two years old when Jade had died. Over the years, I did share with her a memory book I had created. In it was a picture of Jade, her footprints, many beautiful cards, other mementos and poems written by members of our family as well as one I had written.

Angel Sister

My baby sister is an angel
in the heavens above.
She visits me often.
We share moments I love.

She played with me
in the garden today.
I chased the butterflies
as she sent them my way.

When the wind blew softly,
I closed my eyes.
I could feel her sweet kisses.

What a beautiful surprise.

Oops! I tripped over a rock
That I did not see.
But, she caught me gently,
So I didn't skin my knee.

I got up quickly and said,
"I'm okay."
"Thank you angel sister
for saving the day."

Soon a little bird
started singing to me.
I sat back down
and listened carefully.

The song was a message
from the heavens above.
Sent by my sister,
my angel, with love.

She wanted to say
how much fun it had been,
seeing me smile
and hearing me laugh once again.

She said my dear sister
I know sometimes you are sad
That you can't see or hear me
As you can with mom and dad.

But know that I love you
And, I'm always right there.
We can hug in your dreams.
And, your prayers I can hear.

Written for Reagan in memory of Jade

I recorded what happened because I was just so amazed at our daughter's level of understanding and the grace that directed our present conversation. I was at home after finally being discharged from the hospital. It had been five days since we had seen each other. She climbed up onto the bed and said, "Mommy, I had a bad dream last night." When I asked what she dreamt, she said, "you were in the hospital and you died." All I could manage to say was, "I'm sorry you had such a bad dream." I then said, "Daddy and I have something important we need to talk to you about."

I told her that Jackson died. Her first response was, "Really mommy?" When we both said yes, she asked, "Are you sure?" My husband said, "He's not in mommy's tummy anymore." She had been sitting on the bed, but then laid beside me. I asked her if she wanted to know anything else. She said "yes," but then didn't ask or say anything else. I said to her, "you can ask anything you want to." She then asked, "What happened?" I said "he was born too early." She just laid quietly, then turned her back to us.

After two or three minutes passed, with her back still turned, she said "Daddy, you can go now." My husband and I looked at each other and then he left. She turned to me and said, "Mommy, I'm so sorry that Jackson died." She started to cry and so did I. She immediately stopped crying and asked me not to cry. I explained that it was okay to cry when you feel sad or see others cry. She insisted that she did not want me to cry. I realized that this was her way of saying that she couldn't bear to see me hurting.

She then asked, "What day was I born?" I said her complete birth date. Then she asked about Jade's birthday and then Jackson's. She remarked, "We were all in the 2000's." I responded "yes." She immediately sat up and excitedly said, mommy if Jade was alive and Jackson was alive, you would have three kids, wouldn't that be great?" I said "yes." She then said, "but it's okay mommy because now Jade isn't alone anymore. She and Jackson can play with each other in heaven and you have me." I smiled and said "yes, I am thankful for you."

She laid back down and said "maybe you can have another baby." I said, "I don't think so honey." Her response was "you can keep having more babies and more babies until they all run out." I couldn't help but laugh out loud. At some point, she also said that when she's a grownup maybe she can have a baby and give it to me. She wanted so much to comfort me.

Throughout that first week, she would often say, "I'm sorry Jackson died." She did ask if she could tell her teachers that her brother died. I said "yes." She asked if she could tell her friends. When I said that maybe she shouldn't because that might make them sad, her response was, "but I don't want them to be happy thinking that my brother is still coming." I simply said, "Okay."

Irma had knitted a blanket intended for Jackson and asked if she could give it to Reagan. She placed it around Reagan's shoulders and told her that Jackson's love was in the blanket. Reagan was unusually quiet during Irma's visit. Then as Irma was leaving, Reagan went to hug her and simply said, "I love you."

That evening as we were sitting on the couch, Reagan decided that we should snuggle in the blanket together. She asked if we could say that Jade's love was in the blanket too. I said that we could and she was very content. I was very touched by Irma's gesture and was amazed at Reagan's reaction.

In the weeks that followed, I was grateful for many thoughtful persons and I accepted much help. I had learned the importance of allowing others to be there during difficult times. There were no words that could ease the pain, but I found comfort in their loving intentions.

Accepting help had become much easier especially given my time on bed rest. Asking for help, however, did not come as easily, until now. My weakened physical state made it necessary to ask for help in order to meet my family's needs while I regained my health. Family and friends and neighbors were very willing to be a constant source of love as well as wonderful meals.

The gratitude I felt for avoiding both organ failure and a hysterectomy seemed to delay the shock of all that had occurred. As I became physically stronger, my emotions became more fragile. I know that my fluctuating hormones were also a factor. But my past experience with grief had shown me that I just had to face whatever came and live through it as best I could.

Growth Journal entry dated January 13, 2010.....................

Today is a real struggle. The pain I'm feeling is heart-break…a sensation all too familiar, but no easier. Right now I wish that there was a fast-forward button that I could push and be transposed beyond this intense pain. I'm finding it very difficult to focus on what-is rather than what could have been. I'm doing the best that I can to be patient and take each day as it comes. It's really hard to do. I did not expect to be in this place again. It's seems so unfair. If this is my chosen path, then why can't I choose normalcy and predictability for the remainder of my life? But, what is normal? I know a life without pain is impossible. I know that these tears won't last forever. I can deal with uncertainty. I just need to know that everything is for a greater good. If not, what's the point of it all? I feel really drained. I trust that I will get through this...

Growth Journal entry dated January 16, 2010.............. *A few days ago, I wrote that I didn't expect to be in the same place I was four years ago. I am faced with the familiar feeling that there is much I have no control over. Still, I recognize that I am not the same person. I accept more readily that pain and struggles are a great part of life. It seems that just as a butterfly has to struggle out of its cocoon in order to fly, I have had to experience loss in order to grow. I know it couldn't have happened any other way. Nevertheless, it is still painful.*

ANSWER: Pain and loss are part of the human experience. Believe that you can emerge stronger and with greater compassion. Live through the difficult days as best you can. Reach out to those trusted people who love you and are honored to walk with you during sad times. Comfort is a gift of grace. Learn how to receive it.

Chapter 5

In New Light

I was transferred from the surgical intensive care unit back to the maternity floor late in the day on January 2nd. One of the doctors who had been in the operating room came to see me. His words were, "we don't know what happened, but you're still here because you were healthy." All I could say was, "Thank you." I didn't feel the need to ask any questions.

Hearing the words *you're still here because you were healthy* immediately began to restore trust in my body. For a long time, I felt as though this body that I took such good care of had failed me. This doctor affirmed that my body survived a serious emergency situation because I was in good health. For the first time in a long while, I recognized that my body had served me well.

The intubation process had caused irritation to the muscles in the back of my throat resulting in moderate apnea. I would fall asleep and then suddenly wake up gasping for air. This caused me to spend many hours lying awake just trying to make sense of all that had happened. This night, I was praying, thanking God not only for allowing me to pull through, but also for allowing me to survive without having a hysterectomy. As grateful as I was, I was still in a familiar place of deep sorrow. I needed assurance that everything would truly be okay. I asked God to *please show me the way through this.* Within minutes of this prayer, I received a text message from my best childhood friend. It was shortly after midnight when I received her text.

I immediately called to ask what caused her to send me the text at that exact moment. She said that she had written it about four o'clock that afternoon. We had spoken earlier that evening, but she never mentioned it. She explained that given everything I had been through, she was unsure if it was appropriate to send. So, she saved it.

Then for no apparent reason, she decided to send it just after midnight. It was to let me know that her offer to be a gestational surrogate was still an option and to consider it. She had first made this offer almost exactly two years earlier. I had emphatically said, "No." I remember saying that *a child should be created out of love.* At that time, there was no reason to think that I would never be able to carry a child to term. And, never before had my life been threatened.

I discussed this with my obstetrician who came to see me the next morning. She shared how a good friend had used a gestational carrier to have a child. She said that ending up in the ICU was reason enough not to attempt another pregnancy. She didn't think that anything else could be done to insure a different outcome given my history. I explained that my husband and I had previously agreed that this would be our final attempt. She understood and advised that using a gestational carrier was a valid option.

Still, in the weeks that followed, doubt crept in. I wrote in an email to a friend on Monday, January 18, 2010:

I have been moving away from the idea of having my cousin be a gestational carrier. The hope of having another child warms my heart and in some ways eases my sorrow; yet, I know how much that growing child comes to mean to you. I don't think that I can ask one of my dearest friends to carry a child for 9 months and then give that child to me, no matter the biology. No matter how pure her intentions, she will be experiencing a loss on some level. So, I pray for the conviction to make the most unselfish decision for the sake of all involved.

Then, on February 1, 2010, I recorded the following dream:

I am in an unfamiliar place, yet it feels like it could be my home. I know that I am waiting for someone. It is not clear who I'm waiting for. I feel anxious. Then, I hear a gentle knock at the door. I go to the door, but stand there in silence. I wait. I make no attempt to open the door. I don't ask who's there or try to see who it is. I just stand there. Then, the voice says, "It is me." This is when I open the door.

This dream helped me to realize where I was in my life. I was very hesitant to open any door until I was certain I wouldn't be disappointed. But, I knew that absolute certainty did not exist.

When I met with Irma a few days later, I shared all that I was living. She helped me to clearly see that I had more discerning to do before I could reach a final decision. She also cautioned to be patient with myself. I needed to allow myself much time and healing before making any major decisions. I heeded her advice and shifted my attention for the time being.

I mentioned in the last chapter, Doreen Virtue's Archangel Oracle Cards and the two cards which I selected from the deck on the morning of Jackson's burial. At that time, I couldn't understand the relevance of the card that read, Teaching and Learning, Archangel Zadkiel: "Keep an open mind and learn new ideas. Then, teach these ideas to others."

It was towards the end of February that I realized the significance of this card. On the final day of the workshop, *Leading My Life*, I wrote;

> *I feel it is no coincidence that I was able to take this workshop. Yes, I have been looking for assurance that my life experiences have not been random and meaningless. But, there has been something else. It's a sense of a greater purpose beyond my own needs. Am I intended to help others on a similar path to healing?*

> *A few weeks ago, I began to say the words of the San Damiano Prayer by Saint Francis of Assisi which reads,*

> *Most High and glorious God,*
> *Lighten the darkness of my heart.*
> *Give me sound faith,*
> *Firm hope,*
> *And perfect love.*
> *Give me, Oh God,*
> *The right feelings and knowledge,*
> *So that I may carry out the task*
> *That you have given me in truth.*
> *-Saint Francis of Assisi*

The first time I recited this prayer, I again felt a stirring inside. It wasn't anxiety or excitement, but it was something rising from within that I still can't quite name. That day, I started a book about leaning on God through the storm. It referenced a biblical passage, Mark 1: 16-20, where Jesus asks Simon and Andrew to become fishers of men. As grace would have it, this was the same sermon at church that Sunday. So, I began to pay even more attention to this calling.

Today, it's even more apparent. When I began this process of inner work, it was intended for my own personal growth and healing. Now, there is a growing desire to help others recognize that they have within them all that is needed to move beyond their struggles and live life more fully. It requires awareness, healing, silence and guidance to reach this place of inner wisdom.

Soon after this workshop, I began the training process of becoming a PRH educator in order to help people in their growth and healing. That "stirring," I can now name. It was the intuition that I was created to live a life of giving love and nurturing others that extended beyond my own family.

Andre Rochais, the founder of PRH, firmly believed that each person holds within them unique gifts that are essential for all of society to evolve. By committing to the process of growth and methodically exploring their inner world, each person would ultimately come to recognize the true meaning of their life.

"We are asleep on a goldmine, on a
wellspring of energy, on a volcano of
creativity. Everything is there, in the
hidden corners of Humanity, in the
interior recesses of men and women
throughout the planet."
-Andre Rochais

Growth Journal entry dated November 19, 2010..................
What is it that I am grateful for today? Something aside from the obvious…
life, my family, my friends. I am grateful for… technology and science. I've
always loved science. I think because of the reliability in predicting specific
outcomes. Now, I realize that there is so much science cannot explain or
predict. There is so much that remains a mystery. I am left feeling that
there is more to who I am. I am more than this body. I am an expression
of love. My heart is full, but no longer heavy. There is a lightness which
feels peaceful and joyous. I want others to feel this peace. If only we could
all recognize that our truest purpose is to love and be loved. This would
solve so much conflict. This saddens me…conflict, hurt, disrespect for
others. I desire to be a part of the healing.

Life's Messages: Pay attention to the stirring from within even
if you are not yet able to name it. See your intuition as a conveyor
of light. Allow that inner sense to direct you even when the path
seems unclear or uncertain.

Chapter 6

Changing Directions

Difficult circumstances often crack the shell of our day to day lives. When life is no longer as usual, we are open to seeing what matters most even if we are not the ones directly affected. My cousin who made the offer to be a gestational carrier began the process of re-evaluating her own life soon after my ordeal. She is a single mom and was living in another state at the time. We had often talked about her moving closer in hope that our girls would have a bond similar to what we shared. We have been close friends for almost thirty years. Whether or not we decided to move forward with the surrogacy, it was definitely a shared desire to be physically closer. She decided to put her house up for sale and see what would happen.

Towards the end of April, she sold her house with a closing date of June 25th. We marveled at how everything fell into place, allowing this move to truly happen. It was a sure sign that this was the way it was meant to be. Now that she would be living here, I started to revisit the idea of gestational surrogacy. My husband was obviously open to exploring this option. So, we began to research this process. I met with a social worker to find out how these cases were typically handled.

Growth Journal entry dated May 18, 2010...........................
Today, I met with a social worker to learn more about the surrogacy process. What do I feel? I am completely overwhelmed. There are so, so many thoughts. She made it all seem so possible. When my eyes filled with tears, I knew that this was something I was willing to look further into. But, if this had not been an option, I would have made peace by now with the fact that I would have an only child. But, it is an option. Had I not received my cousin's text within minutes of asking God to show me the way through all this, I probably wouldn't be considering this. But, if it was meant to happen, why has it not happened the way nature intended it? The way nature intended? I remember when I first said "no" to this idea; I said that I wanted my child to be created out of love. And then about a month later, I learned the circumstances of my conception. I was definitely not created out of romantic love. So, there went that idealistic view. If I'm being completely honest with myself, I have to admit that I have been trying to suppress the idea of moving forward with this process because of fear...fear of more disappointment. We've been through so much already. But, if there is another child to be born to me without risking my life, how could I not explore this option?

Looking back at this entry, it seems that there were a multitude of "buts." I could see the conflict that I was experiencing. Taking a logical, mental approach only led me around in circles. During this time, the words "keep an open mind" began to echo. First, I came across a quote by Helen Keller that read;

> *"When one door of happiness closes, another opens;*
> *but often we look so long at the closed door that we*
> *do not see the one which has opened for us."*

I remember staring at these words in disbelief. This is obviously a beautiful quote, but the timing of it was incredible. Then, I was discarding some old college notes and stumbled upon this phrase;

"Even if I knew that tomorrow the world would go to pieces, I would still plant my apple tree." -Dr. Martin Luther King, Jr.

This would be a definite path of uncertainty, but considering the possible outcome, well worth it.

Still, it wasn't until November 2010 that I finally met with a specialist to discuss the option of assisted reproduction and the gestational surrogacy process. My husband had already come to the decision that this was a valid option for us. It was easy for him because my life was not being placed at risk. In his words, "a no-brainer." So, I decided to take this first meeting alone. During this consultation, I recognized that there was still a part of me that was hoping this doctor would say that it was still possible for me to carry a baby to term. He didn't.

Growth Journal entry dated November 3, 2010..................
Tears begin to well up in me as I think about the fact that I could never again safely carry a child. I knew this before now. But, today it really sank in. It saddens me. It feels like a dream that was unrealized...a prayer that went unanswered. So, now I have to accept this reality that feels so heavy right now. I am a mother at the very depths of my core. This is what I was created for...to love children unconditionally...to trust in their goodness... to believe in them...to keep them safe as best I could...to guide them in becoming who they are meant to be without judgment, with enough freedom so that I too can learn what they are meant to teach me. I don't know where this process will lead, but I trust that this is the direction I

am meant to go in. The doctor's words now echo, "The odds are in your favor." As I shift my focus to this new possibility, I am filled with hope. I know there's still much to consider. Even with the uncertainty, the path now seems clearer. It feels like a yes. A soft yes.

Growth Journal entry dated February 3, 2011...............*After months of much thought, research, consultations and prayer, I have decided to move forward with something I never dreamt I would. In fact, it is something I initially said no to. I have made the decision to accept my best childhood friend's offer to be a gestational carrier in hopes of my husband and I having another child. This decision leaves me feeling hopeful, happy and excited about the possibility. While there are no guarantees, we've never had a problem conceiving, so as the doctor put it, the odds are in our favor. Now as we begin the actual process, there is a part of me left wondering if this is truly divinely guided when there is so much medical intervention and decision-making? There have been many instances in my life where I have made decisions based on a sense of knowing that that this was meant to be. But, none have required so much thought and planning......*

The series of legal, psychological and medical steps leading up to this process seemed enormous. While my cousin's one and only pregnancy had been uncomplicated, she still had to undergo thorough evaluations and much testing to determine if she was a good candidate for gestational surrogacy and that she would not be taking any undo risks, "medically or emotionally." I could have never asked this of her, but felt overwhelmingly grateful for her willingness to endure this process even after learning about what it truly involved. Because of this deep gratitude, I was very surprised that certain feelings would arise in me.

Growth Journal entry dated February 9, 2011..............*What is most alive in me at this moment? Right now my left shoulder and wrist hurts. It's because I slipped and fell on the ice while walking Logan. Jenaire came out and said she'd walk him. I didn't want her to fall and hurt herself, but she insisted. She walked him and she didn't fall. Why is this bothering me so much? This is ridiculous. There's something deeper here. I am so grateful for everything she is doing for me; yet, there's a feeling of why can she do this, but not I? Whoa. This is unexpected. The psychologist that we saw separately and then together raised many valid issues, but these feelings never came up. It seems child-like to ask, why can she, but not I? But it's not ridiculous. When I go to that place of non-judgment, it feels like a very human thing to do. It's really hard for me to let go of something I've wanted for so long. The idea of "sharing" a pregnancy is not what I ever imagined...Be gentle with yourself. You did the best you could. You did all that you could. It wasn't meant to happen the way you imagined, but it can still happen. This is the voice I now hear. This is the voice I want to listen to. I acknowledge that I wish that I could be the one to carry this pregnancy. But, now when I imagine holding a baby in my arms, I don't feel as though it will truly matter how this baby came to be, especially when this baby will actually be a part of me. Okay. I feel okay with this. My shoulder and wrist still hurt, but I feel more at peace. For this I am grateful.*

This was the most life-altering decision I have ever had to make. While it was not solely my decision, I needed to feel completely at peace. Even after coming to a decision, it was still important that I verify that I could live with this decision no matter what. I had to consult with each pivotal center as taught in PRH; my being or deepest self, my sensibility or level of emotions, my body and then my intellect.

At the level of my Being, this decision seemed rooted in my unwavering certitude of deep love that is lived with mothering. It was also in full accord with my faith and trust in the goodness of life.

At the level of my emotional zone, I felt that I was able to endure the uncertainty of this process. There was a sensation of wonderment—an extraordinary sense of being led in this specific direction. It felt right within me. What was once a soft yes, seemed much louder.

At the level of my body, I felt excited about the possibility and was willing to endure all the medical procedures without much apprehension. This was huge for me. I am careful about what goes into my body. In my entire adult life, I cannot recall ever using a single over-the-counter medication prior to this process. I had never before taken birth control pills or used any medication on a regular basis. It was important for me to recognize that my body was up for this challenge.

My intellect was also in alignment with this. It was interesting to no longer view conception as solely a natural process and begin to view in vitro fertilization as miraculous. I was confident that this was the best decision I could make and I was willing to see it through.

This decision seemed to be in line with my deep conscience, the inner compass that guides persons in the pursuit of complete fulfillment. There were many reasons not to move forward with this complicated process. But, this decision was not based on logic or what others thought I should do. When I considered the idea of saying no, I felt disheartened and clearly not at peace. At the very least, it felt important to walk through this door that had opened up to me.

Life's Messages: While seeking reassurance that you are on the right path, remain open to the myriad of possibilities. There is more than one door to life and multiple paths to happiness. Live and act from your deepest self. Remain true to what is essential in you.

Chapter 7

A New Dream

For as long as I can remember, I have had a fascination with dreams and their interpretations. I was in my early teens when I had a dream about seeing a crib on a sandy beach. Inside the crib was a fish. This was during the summer which was spent in my grandmother's care. When I told her about this dream, she declared that it meant that someone was pregnant. *Because I dreamt of a crib?* I had asked. "No," she said. It was because of the fish. Soon after, I learned that one of my teen cousins was indeed pregnant.

Before I knew that I was pregnant with Reagan, I dreamt of fish swimming in the sky. Some days later, I took a home test which was positive. I immediately recalled my grandmother's interpretation of fish in dreams. This became the way my inner voice communicated to me that I was pregnant. Then one day I was surprised that I was not pregnant after such a dream. I later learned that one of my sisters was pregnant.

While this type of dream offered me clear and instant insight, other dreams seem to be a strange mix of events of the day combined with my fears or expectations. I don't record every dream, but I do make it a point to remember the ones that leave me completely baffled. Much later, I would come to understand their significance.

One of these dreams occurred before I became pregnant with our son, Jackson. I dreamt that my husband and I were at a stadium. A woman had given birth to sextuplets and was about to select six couples from the crowd to give each of her babies to. We were the third couple to be chosen. This woman chose us to be parents to a newborn boy that she had given birth to. After learning that I was pregnant with a boy, I thought about this dream. As we began the gestational surrogacy process, this dream took on a whole different meaning.

God's imagination is greater than anything you could ever dream. In recent weeks, I have heard this phrase repeatedly from different sources. When I hear the same message, I tend to pay attention. Still, it has taken much time to replace my dream of giving birth to another child with anything other than that. It has been my dream for many years. My extensive history of unexplained miscarriages, premature deliveries and the complications that followed my last delivery has made pregnancy a "clear medical contraindication" for me. I had no other choice but to let go of that dream.

After all the evaluations, testing and counseling sessions, we began the process of synchronizing our cycles. The irony of taking birth control pills as a means to achieving a pregnancy seemed quite odd although I understood the reason. Our cycles needed to be in close proximity so that when eggs were retrieved from me and then fertilized, her body would be adequately prepared to maintain the pregnancy.

We both had to endure the process of injecting ourselves with medications. The medications I received were intended to ripen a number of my eggs to increase the chances of successful fertilization, while her medications were intended to suppress ovulation and prepare her uterus so that the embryo would implant successfully. During this time, we were both closely monitored with blood tests and pelvic ultrasounds. On one of my visits, I recall the technician's words, "your ovaries are blossoming."

The egg retrieval took place on April 5, 2011. I found this procedure to be most unnerving because it would require sedation. As I was brought into the procedure room, I silently prayed that this medication would do only what it needed to and nothing more. The actual process took only 15-20 minutes. I awoke in the recovery room without complications and was informed that they had successfully retrieved a good number of eggs—Twenty three to be exact.

The next step after fertilization was to see which embryos would continue to grow and be selected for transfer. An embryologist, a specially trained laboratory scientist would assess the embryos to determine which of them had the highest probability of implanting in the uterus and result in pregnancy. Some embryos reach approximately 100 cells over the course of four or five days and are then referred to as a blastocyst. Blastocysts have an even greater chance of implantation. We were also aware that on occasion, no embryos are viable for embryo transfer.

We would only be doing this once. That was the plan. If it was meant to be, I was confident that it would happen at the first attempt. We had already been through so much disappointment and I couldn't imagine repeated treatment cycles. The timing was right and I felt as though this was truly divinely guided.

At the time of our meeting to sign the consent forms, I was opposed to the idea of any embryos being frozen. I was adamant about only trying this once. My husband helped me to see that it was reasonable to have any remaining embryos frozen, just in case. He said that I may feel differently later on. I reluctantly agreed, but hoped that this wouldn't be the case. I never really focused on this. I truly tried to approach this process one step at a time.

On the morning of April 10th, we received the call to confirm that a transfer would occur. The best case scenario would have been to transfer a single embryo, but no more than two. A single embryo had reached the blastocyst stage and was selected to be transferred. I was thankful that this decision was so clear-cut.

Everything went according to plan that morning. The developing embryo was placed into my cousin's uterus by means of a catheter inserted through the cervix and guided by ultrasound. She reached out to hold my hand during this process. To quote the doctor who performed the transfer, "so far, so good." I was given an ultrasound printout of the blastocyst and given the date of our pregnancy test, which was April 22nd, Good Friday. This date felt significant.

For the next eleven days, I kept hoping that I would dream of fish. I struggled to remember the details of many dreams during this time, but I was pretty sure that I didn't have any fish dreams. I've always, always remembered them. This was definitely a lesson in patience. For the first time, I would have to wait to find out. We agreed not to take a home pregnancy test and just wait for the official word.

Between the time of the transfer and the pregnancy test, I received a letter stating that two additional embryos had continued to grow on the day of the transfer and were frozen. Now that there were two additional embryos, I began to feel a bit unsettled. I had said I would only do this once, but now couldn't fathom the idea of these embryos just being destroyed. They were a part of me. My cousin assured me that she would be willing to this again. This helped to shift my focus back to the current pregnancy.

Around 2pm on Friday, one of the nurses called with the results of the pregnancy test. It was negative. I felt my heart drop. I knew they were no guarantees, but I hadn't really considered this possibility. I didn't allow myself to think about anything other than a positive outcome. *How could I be led in this direction for no reason?*

The following morning I awoke in tears. I couldn't understand the intensity of my emotions. So, I wrote and this is what poured out:

> I didn't feel you growing inside me,
> But I felt you in my soul.
> This time, I did not hold you,
> But I held you in my heart.
>
> There is a deep sense of loss
> Because I hoped that you would be.
> For a brief moment,
> you were.
>
> It is hard to think a part of me has died.
> I would rather believe that a part of me lived.
> Because if you lived,
> then you are most certainly still alive.

I did not expect that I would feel the pain of this disappointment so deeply, but I could not deny the hurt. The sadness I felt was no different than previous losses. I was grieving yet another loss.

Where there was firm hope,
There is now deep disappointment.
Where there was much peacefulness,
There is now great sadness.

Where there was love,
There is still love.
God's love, your love, my love.

With this love,
Hopefulness will return.
With this love,
Peacefulness will resume.
This I know is true.

I have heard many times that from the moment of conception, we have everything within us that makes us who we are. In that instant, our physical characteristics, our growth, the aging process, even our dispositions are all set in motion. Never before had I considered that the existence of tiny cells was indeed a life. This process awakened my deep connection to and respect for all of life even in its earliest stages.

Life's Messages: Some dreams come true, while others do not. Learn how to gently replace your unrealized dreams with new ones. Though you may find it hard to believe, there is often something greater beyond what you could ever imagine. Continue to trust.

Chapter 8

Terre Nouvelle

A week later, I was headed to Canada to spend a weekend at a retreat center called Terre Nouvelle. The English translation is "New Earth." This center was created about twenty-five years ago by a group of retired PRH educators who shared Andre Rochais' vision of bringing about fundamental changes in society through the growth of the human person. I did not know what to expect when I first arrived. My only hope was to spend much time in silence and connecting with my inner world.

I was back in my modest accommodations that Friday evening. As I drifted off to sleep, I had a vision of talking with one of the male participants I had not yet spoken with. I envisioned him speaking of the country of Trinidad, which is where my biological father originated. I was not fully asleep, so this caused me to be more awake. For a while after, thoughts of my biological father entered my mind. I wondered if he ever thought of or spoke of me. He was a much older man, a friend to one of my mother's brother-in-laws. For years, the only facts I knew about him was his name and where he was from. Then in March of 2009, I learned the circumstances surrounding my conception and birth.

In my search to better understand my truest nature, I wanted to know about my parentage. So, for the first time ever, I asked.

I was told that he knew I existed and even saw me once, as an infant. I also learned that he had other children who were about my mom's age at the time of my birth. Everything I ever fantasized that he could be, he was not. Why was this entering my consciousness at this particular time and in this particular place? As I write this, it has been over 10 years since his passing.

This gentleman who had been in my vision approached me at breakfast the next morning and we struck up a conversation. I mentioned that I was originally from the Caribbean and he talked about having friends from Trinidad. The mere mention of Trinidad stunned me. This experience and my time at Terre Nouvelle prompted the following writing.

A Letter to My...

What of you is in me? I exist because of you. So, by definition, you are my father. I never knew you although you knew of me. I do not love you, but I don't despise you either. It makes me sad to know that I was not created out of love. How is it that I can love so deeply in spite of this? I was not loved by you, but I was loved. I was not created out of your love, but I was created out of God's love. My hope is that the best of you is in me. That is all. Goodnight.

I soon recognized that just being in this environment, surrounded by a like-minded community of people would awaken my intuition and bring about much insight. Without knowing my story, another workshop participant said to me, "my word for you would be fertility." This was right after I had shared the following reflection with members of a smaller group. The writing exercise was to focus on exploring our unique contribution to the world.

Reflective Writing, April 30, 2011....*Love is most alive in me at this very moment. I love deeply. I care wholeheartedly. I love life. This earth. This place where every person and every thing has a place. I was meant to be here. I was meant to create life. I am a mother...a source of life. It's no wonder I feel called to help the life in others emerge fully. In this moment, I realize that grief and loss were a necessary part of allowing the life within me to break through. I have finally taken hold of that life from deep within me that has been reaching out. Now that I am more rooted, I now seek to help others become whole. I recognize that I can only be a facilitator of healing for others. It is their innate potential that will allow them to fully heal.*

When he used the word *fertility,* he commented that he got the sense that there is something extraordinary that has been planted in me. I was very touched by this sentiment. From an early age, the desire to be of service to humanity seemed to be very much alive in me. When I look back at my earliest journal, my "Daisy Day" diary, I am struck by the words I wrote at the age of fifteen. On July 20, 1989, I wrote that *I wish to give something to this world... There are so many things I need to understand. When and how I will understand them, I don't know. Only God knows what's in store for me.* Even then, I was certain that a higher power would lead me in my mission to serve humanity.

One of our workshop activities on Sunday morning involved walking the many acres of land at Terre Nouvelle in silence. Our instructions were to explore the land, guided by spontaneity, simplicity and child-like innocence. When we returned from the walk, we were then to allow ourselves to be attracted with this same spontaneity to the creative expression materials available to us. We were to invent, play and have fun. After completing our artwork, we were given guidelines for reflective writing.

Reflective Writing, April 30, 2011….*As I walked the land, I felt free. I imagined myself as a young child, skipping and jumping and running through the open field. I eventually made my way over to the pine tree forest. I stood in one spot, looking up at the rays of sunlight peering through. I was alone with no one else in sight, yet I felt fearless. I closed my eyes and allowed my heart to become full with this brilliant light. A deep sense of love erupted within me. Love for the beauty and wonders of life. For all that I am and for all that I am becoming. There is a desire for others to share in this light. I wish for others to become whole. We all have the potential to heal, to grow, to become all that we were intended and heal our broken earth, which has been crying out to us. She too wants to be healed. I see myself as the tiny heart at the center of my artwork, giving rise to others hearts of varying sizes. If I can plant my seed of love and encourage others to do the same, miraculous things can occur. Out of love comes healing. I know this is true. While this isn't new for me, it is a confirmation of my truest purpose.*

One of the retreat attendees was a physician from Belgium. During the sharing in smaller groups, she was drawn to the fact that I constructed what appeared to be a branch with three leaflets on the right and a branch with two leaflets on the left. She was struck by the fact that I placed them on the sides that accurately corresponded with the tricuspid valve on the right side of the heart and the bicuspid valve on the left side of the heart. Even my arbitrary cutting and pasting resulted in a representation of the heart. It was amazing to see how something I created without any plan or thought brought so much insight.

As I look again at this creative expression, I am drawn to the colors I chose. I notice that I encircled the tiny heart in the center with a series of concentric circles with a shade of deep blue. I've known for quite some time that blue symbolized peace. I recently read that dark blue symbolized truth. It is important for me to know what is true, so that I may live and share that truth. I also see this small, central heart as the love implanted in me by my grandparents who met and fell in love on an island once called "heart."

My trip to Terre Nouvelle was timely, fruitful and enjoyable. There was much that had been awakened in me. I left with a greater understanding of the community dimension of the Being. It is the aspect of our deepest self that allows us to connect with others who share the same core values and a similar mission.

Reflective Writing, April 31, 2011...*Terre Nouvelle. It is here that I have been able to see that although I was not created out of romantic love, I was created out of God's love. There is a sense of belonging—of coming home. I feel a connection, not only to this group, but to others who wish to become whole and facilitate the healing of this beautiful earth. Drinking from the wellspring this weekend deepened my connection and love for the earth and for all of humanity. I am like an obedient child, but no longer out of fear. This obedience is due to my trust in the goodness of life and in our compassion as human beings. We were all given gifts unique to our journey—Gifts that were not intended to be kept hidden away. These treasures were meant to be unearthed and intended for us to share.*

Life's Messages: Seek out groups or practices that encourage you to explore your inner world. Surround yourself with life-giving people. Know that you were created out of Divine love and that you have Divine purpose.

Chapter 9

Trying Again

"Let yourself live and be in each moment, with each lesson along the way. Destiny isn't some place we go. Destiny is where you are."
-Melody Beattie

It takes great strength and courage to try again after painful and repeated disappointments, but the decision to move forward with a second embryo transfer was not a difficult one. Life had already been created and our only option was to see this process through. This time we decided to transfer both of the remaining embryos. Our hope was that both would implant or at the very least, we would increase the "odds" of achieving a successful pregnancy.

This time there were no injections or medications on my part. It still took about six weeks for my cousin to undergo the process of preparing her uterus for the transfer. We were told that not every embryo survived the thawing process or is suitable for transfer. This was truly another lesson in letting go. With each day, there came a greater awareness that the only absolute certainty was the right here and the right now.

In the time leading up to the first transfer, I had no doubt that I would produce viable eggs that would be fertilized. I did everything that was asked of me and I had been clear about what I wanted. Still, we did not get the desired outcome. This time I could not be sure that either of these remaining embryos would survive the thawing process. This time there was even more uncertainty. This time I truly understood what it meant to surrender completely. There was simply too much that was beyond my control.

Growth Journal entry dated June 13, 2011....................... *My thoughts today are focused on the transfer. We should get the call soon to say whether or not it will still happen. What dwells in me at this time is a sense of hope. Faith and hope are all that I have when nothing else is for certain. I can't imagine that I was led down this road for no reason. It is my greatest desire to be a mother again. So, I trust that this is the way it is meant to happen. There is one other lesson that I am quite certain that I have learned. From this point on, I will be cautious about how I use the word, never. I had said never to this entire process. I had said that I would never do this again. And, here I am. It seems that when I use that word, life gives me an opportunity to prove myself wrong.*

The morning of the scheduled transfer, we received the call that we were to come in earlier. I did not ask, why, or any other questions. I just trusted that all was well. On our way to the center, my cousin turns and asks me, "So, what did you and God talk about today?" I said, I only asked that God be present in all this. This time I didn't ask for any particular outcome.

Along the way, we talked about how she too had been more relaxed this time around. She had been less strict about the exact timing of the medications and her test results had still been great.

She was also less nervous about this transfer having experienced it before.

When we arrived, a nurse explained that they were running about an hour and fifteen minutes behind. We left to have lunch and returned an hour later. We still had a lengthy wait. This was in stark contrast to the first transfer where everything was done on time and went as planned with the exception of a favorable outcome. In keeping with the idea of Universal balance, I could only hope that this time there would be a different outcome...a positive one.

Again, I was given an ultrasound picture of a blastocyst. The procedure went well. My comment to the nurse was, "I assume the other embryo did not survive the thawing process." She looked at me questioningly and while I can't recall her exact words, I am pretty sure they were *what other embryo?* I explained to her that there should have been two embryos. When my records were reviewed by the attending doctor, we learned that only one embryo had been thawed. She proceeded to contact the original doctor who was handling my case. After a few moments, she returned to say that he would call me after reviewing my chart. She assured me that he is very meticulous and would "get to the bottom of this."

On the ride home, my cousin and I were mainly quiet. Not only had it been an exhausting day, but we were also immersed in our own thoughts. At some point, she said "of all the people this could have happened to." I said to her, "I only asked that God be present. So, I will trust that He was present."

About five o'clock that evening I received the call from my doctor. He explained that there had been a miscommunication and that this has never happened before. He assumed full responsibility. I calmly said, "I am disappointed, but I do believe whatever is meant to be, will be." He seemed shocked by my response. He said, "It seems that I am more upset about this than you are." I assured him that I was very disappointed because I had expected this to be our final attempt, but "it is what it is" and I accepted his apology. He also offered to cover the expense of a subsequent transfer and wished me luck with the current pregnancy attempt.

I truly believed that God had been present, so there was no need to be angry. I was disappointed because again everything did not work out as I thought it would. I could have easily seen this situation as another test of faith. However, I now see how much my inner quality of faith has unfolded and emerged as I have learned to trust in each experience.

Life's Messages: If it is time for you to receive what you have been hoping for, trust that it will happen. If the timing is still not right, learn the lessons along the way. Trust that no part of the journey is without purpose.

Chapter 10

An Extraordinary Revelation

"Trust the light that shines within."
-Snatam Kaur

On the morning of June 17th, I wrote in my journal that *I am more open to Divine will in my life and to living more fully my intended path.* This is certainly true. I still keep an intention list and enjoy checking off and writing thank you when that intention becomes a reality. Instead of asking for things to work out according to my plan, I now ask that God be present.

I have often looked upwards and outwards for guidance. There is now a deep sense that I am to look within. Now that I have clearly identified my inner voice through PRH journal writing and my morning practice of Qi Gong, a form of moving meditation, the messages seem to come with greater clarity.

At a recent PRH group meeting, I experienced a guided meditation that was intended to allow each person to connect with the "original child" within. This time for inner reflection differed from past "inner child" meditations in that we were led to the moment of our conception—our pure essence before any external conditioning. We were then to describe this process and the sensations that were awakened.

Reflective Writing, June, 17, 2011.............................. *As I closed my eyes and centered on my breathing, I experienced a sense of lightness...almost as though I was floating. It was with much ease that I began this journey of connecting with my original self. As I was led deeper, there was some resistance as I approached the exact moment of my conception. I felt a sense of panic. This was due to the hurt I imagined my mom was experiencing in that moment. I could not return there. Instead, I forged my way beyond this moment, back to my origination in God's heart. I entered a space of vast darkness. I saw myself as a light and God was cradling me in his palm. A gentle voice said, my child I want to send you into this world. The path may not seem easy, but if you always trust in me and know that you are my child and that I love you, you will become all that you are meant to be. This was overwhelming and brought tears to my eyes. As my tears silently fell, there was a sense of great understanding. It was as though God wanted to be certain that I was ready for this task. God gave me the choice and my original self chose this path. This explains my deep-rooted faith. I've been wondering whether it was an inborn gift or something that was nurtured early on. I now understand my journey...*

I was in bed that night and this meditation continued to repeat in my head. It was unlike any meditation I had experienced before. It was almost like a short movie clip. The analytical part of me wanted to know if was real. It felt real, but I wanted to know without question that it was true.

I received my answer the following day. As a member of the Altar Guild at St. Andrew's Episcopal Church, I prepare the altar for Sunday worship about once every six weeks. This Saturday morning, I prepared the altar as usual and bookmarked the page for Sunday's lesson readings. For the very first time in the six months of doing this, I felt the urge to stop for a moment and read aloud the passage. The passage was Genesis 1:3, *And God said, "Let there be light" and there was light.* I smiled. For me, this was a definite confirmation of the message I had received.

Now as I write this, I see the connection between what I wrote in my journal on the morning of June 17th and this meditation that occurred in the evening of the same day. By stating my openness to Divine will and to living fully my intended path, it is as though I was declaring my readiness to receive this message. And, I did.

Life's Messages: The life within you can provide extraordinary guidance. The answers often emerge more clearly when you are silent and still. Allow time for that stillness to speak.

Chapter 11

Defining Hope

A well meaning person posed the question, 'Why do you say that you are hopeful?" "Why don't you declare to the Universe that this is what you absolutely want?" she also asked. Never before had anyone caused me to question the meaning of hope or more accurately, my interpretation of being hopeful. It felt important to be able to clarify for myself what I truly believed.

When I say *it is my hope*, I am stating my heart's desires at a given time. Naturally, we all want things to work out exactly as we plan. I have also learned to leave an opening for Divine intervention. I realize that there may be possibilities I have yet to consider or otherwise necessary for my soul's journey.

Growth Journal entry dated June 23, 2011...............9:30 a.m. *I am hoping for a positive outcome today. In fact, I suspect that the news today will be good because of the dream I had a few days ago. I dreamt of a sticker of a fish on Jenaire's stomach. It's not my typical fish dream, but it was a fish nonetheless. I wish that I could say that what I feel is pure excitement, but there is some anxiety. It has been such an emotional roller coaster. So, there is no denying my body's tendency to feel nervous. I can't just force myself to think positive. It's not the same as being in a place of peaceful surrender. It feels better to honor my body's response, rather than push these feelings aside. I yearn for another child. It is my greatest desire at this time. It is not easy for me to accept that this is not what is best for me. Yet, I trust in the process of life. Life is good. I trust that I will be able to do all that I am here on this earth to do. This is important to me. Just affirming this makes me feel less anxious. I take deep breaths in order to gently release these feelings of anxiety.*

In the early afternoon on Thursday, June 23rd, the nurse called with the pregnancy test results. I answered the phone in the kitchen. I was alone. I stood still. I caught myself holding my breath as I waited to hear the results after we exchanged greetings. My heart began to race. "We did get a positive," she said, "although the numbers were not as high as we would like to see them." She explained that she has seen numbers like these before that resulted in a live birth and continued to say that we should be, "cautiously optimistic." The test would have to be repeated on Monday to see if the pregnancy hormone levels continued to rise.

As I hung up the phone, I sat on the edge of the kitchen table and just looked out the window. I am an optimist, but I did not know how to do "cautious optimism." I sat quietly for a while and my eyes started to well up with tears. In this moment, there was a good chance that my dream was coming true. So, I chose to honor that. I smiled effortlessly as I delivered the news to my cousin and then to my husband when he returned home, but quickly explained that we needed further confirmation.

I am often satisfied with how calmly I can endure most situations, a gift of docility that has been given to me. But, being on the verge of having the one thing I most desired, it was not easy waiting for more definitive news. Admittedly, it was difficult to stay in the moment. I had to keep reminding myself to shift my thoughts from *what could be* back to *what is*.

I attended a workshop, "Listening to the Messages from My Body" that weekend. An exercise in nature helped me to see how I had been living the surrogacy process. Our instructions were to go outside, be fully present to our breathing and natural walking rhythm and let ourselves be drawn to an object in nature. We were to pick up a stick and spend time holding it tightly, then loosely, and then however we would ordinarily hold it. We were to take note of all we experienced during this exercise that lasted about thirty minutes and then write about it when we returned.

Reflective Writing, June, 26, 2011................................. *The warmth of this beautiful, summer day filled me with joy when I first set out on this walking meditation. I saw a little girl dressed in all pink. She waved to me and I waved back. Further along, I saw a penny and turned it face up, hoping that same little girl might find it. I was drawn to this Y-shaped twig. As I held the twig tightly, I was constantly focused on it and I could feel the tension in my clenched fist during this part of the exercise. I drew a parallel to how I was living this particular stage of the surrogacy process. I have not been able to focus on much else. Everything else seems to be on hold right now. Life is on hold. In this moment, there is some frustration. I can't help but ask, why couldn't this road be a little easier? Why couldn't it have been a definite yes on Thursday? Is this what this y-shaped twig is meant to represent...the constant questioning? When I held the twig loosely, I realized that this also was not the way I wanted to live this process. It matters to me what happens and I want to be present to all of it. I had reached a place of complete surrender throughout the process leading up to the transfer, but I am not able to detach from this specific outcome. Is that even possible in this case? As I held the twig more playfully, I still reflected on the happenings in my life. Still, I noticed that I walked at a slower pace and stopped periodically to observe my surroundings. I watched a little boy walking his dog in the park. He looked about seven. I stopped to ask him his dog's name. I felt concern as I noticed that neither of his parents seemed to be around. I continued on my walk through the park. When I stopped to look back, he was no longer in sight. I sent out a quiet blessing for him to reach home safely and I headed back here. What is most alive in me at the end of this exercise is the remaining concern for that little boy. I can't help but wonder about his living situation. I wonder if his freedom was due to his parents' faith that he could walk through this city park unharmed or was it due to neglect. It is my wish for all children to be safe and loved and nurtured. This ignites the love I have for my own children. I recognize how precious life is. Saying yes to this surrogacy was creating an opportunity for life. I want to believe that this life will get to whatever stage it is meant to. The only way to create this belief is to affirm that everything is as it is supposed to be. Now, as I look at this Y-shaped twig, I wonder, maybe it's meant to represent the letter "Y" in "Yes." Yes to life and to remaining open to all the experiences that life has to teach me. I know it is all for a purpose. I know it is.*

I asked the question whether it is possible to detach from an outcome when the desire is for a child. As I re-read the above reflections, memories of my pregnancy with Reagan begin to flood my mind. I recall that there was some sense of detachment throughout my entire pregnancy with her. Once the pregnancy progressed past 8 weeks, I had no doubt that I would give birth to her; yet, I never consciously communicated with her. I did not express my love for her until she was actually here. In fact, I can recall lying on the operating table and there was a sense of, *is this really happening? Am I really about to become a mother?* I was thirty-four weeks into the pregnancy and had not purchased a single item or prepared a nursery. A patient offered us the use of a crib she no longer needed. That was the only visible sign in our home that we were expecting a much wanted baby.

I kept telling the nurses that I was having incredibly painful contractions, but nothing was registering on the monitors. I'm not a screamer. I had wonderful nurses, but they did not believe my contractions were as strong as they actually were. There was no expectation that my labor would progress that night. My husband had just left to go home. I had told my mother-in-law that she should go as well, but she refused. She was with me when the doctors finally checked my cervix, recognized that labor was imminent and told me that an emergency C-section was my only option. According to the ultrasound that morning, she was measuring only twenty-eight weeks. I was certain that she was about thirty-four weeks, but no less than thirty-three weeks. The tension of the moment by what I was being told and the fact that there were no early ultrasounds caused me to wonder if I could be wrong. *How could I be that much off with my dates? And, what about my dream of fish?* I decided against sharing that piece of information with the attending doctors. My midwife had also been concerned about my measurements and had recommended that I have an ultrasound that was done at or about 24 weeks.

She had also flipped to a breech position with my membranes ruptured. The irony is that there is a chiropractic technique that I have often used to balance the pelvis, which allows a breech baby to turn into a head down position. I never imagined that I would be in this position and not be able to do anything about it. I received local anesthesia because I had eaten only a few hours earlier and the labor had progressed rapidly. So, I was completely aware of everything the doctors were doing. My husband arrived as they were prepping me and my mother-in-law was allowed to stay. I felt incredible pressure which made me nauseous as they did what they could to safely bring my beautiful baby girl into this world.

I did not know the magnitude of a mother's love until I actually held my firstborn in my arms. There is something incredibly majestic about a love for a child that you are ready to love. When those feelings took hold of me, I entered into a new reality. In that moment, I knew I wanted to care for her as best I could. Now that I know how it feels to love a child, it is hard to let go of the outcome.

The pregnancy test was repeated on Monday and the result was negative. For whatever reason, the embryo had stopped developing. Once again, our dreams were crushed. It seems that no matter how often I have experienced this, nothing lessens the pain of loss and disappointment. I just had to allow myself to feel it and yet again, live through it as best I could.

So, how do I continue to hold on to the belief that every disappointment is for a bigger reason? As Robert Brault writes, "If you knew hope and despair were paths to the same destination, which would you choose?" Pain may be inevitable, but I choose to face it, honor my feelings, release the energy of it when I am able to and then allow the experience to move me forward in life. It is the only way I know.

Hearing stories of how other women found their way through grief and loss also offers me hope. At church one Sunday, our pastor invited us to engage in conversation for a few minutes with one person, "a reasonably friendly stranger." As grace would have it, the woman sitting right in front of me had also suffered the loss of a child. She had an infant son and toddler daughter with her. She shared how she had once lost a four year old son to illness. I will never forget her words. She said, "I am blessed to have had him for four years."

On May 31st, 1999, the day of my grandmother's passing, my god-daughter and her twin brother were born sixteen weeks prematurely. They were each one pound at birth. Alec did not survive, but his sister miraculously did. Alexis Miracle is now a healthy 12-year old with no lingering health challenges. Their mom is president and co-founder of Miracle Babies Support Foundation that raises funds to support parents of premature children.

Another woman I met at my women's group also had experienced the searing pain of loss. She had to say goodbye to a three month old daughter, Jayne, due to Sudden Infant Death Syndrome and a four year old son, Raymond, who she lost to Leukemia within two years of each other. She spoke of a letter she wrote to her mother-in-law one snowy, January evening in 1961, just three weeks before her daughter, Jayne died. Her husband had been outside shoveling snow and their five children were snug in their beds. They were living in difficult times and just weeks earlier, they had received a letter from the bank that the mortgage was overdue. Yet, in that moment, she felt that she had "everything that matters in life." She wanted to share that moment of utter and complete joy with someone, so she sat at her dining room table and wrote a letter.

During a recent conversation at that same home, she shared how this feeling is "still alive" in her and she can "almost get the feeling back" when she talks about it. Her mother-in-law kept this precious letter and later returned it to her. In spite of her losses, she expressed her eternal gratitude for that single moment of immeasurable joy. She also said that everything she has ever faced has brought her to a faith beyond what she had known before.

Knowing that others have walked this difficult path and were able to emerge with continued faith has given me much hope. I have also learned that grieving is not a neatly compartmentalized process with a specific timeline. While no one could ever say exactly how long it takes for the fog to lift and for things to make sense again, I have realized that the only way to acceptance is through the pain and chaos. And, that this pain would not last forever.

When we received the disappointing news about the second transfer, the nurse also inquired about our intention to move forward with the final embryo transfer. When she said I did not have to give an immediate answer, I was relieved. I did not have an answer. She said to call when we were ready to begin the process again. About a week later, I prayerfully asked for a sign. I needed Divine guidance to make a decision and a few hours later I heard the song by Kris Allen, "Live Like You're Dying." I sensed that this song held a message. I could have interpreted it to mean that we should not put anything off and immediately go ahead with the final transfer. But when I looked inward, starting the process at this time felt like I would be saying, *okay let's just do it and get it over with*. I did not want to enter this process with that type of energy. So, I had my answer. It felt right to wait. And, that is what we did.

There were other immediate decisions to be made. My husband kept his scheduled appointment for a vasectomy and we made the decision not to freeze any sperm. To continue to travel down this road of assisted reproduction was not what we wanted to endure. So, we are quite certain that there will be one final attempt at having another child. I say "quite" because I have left an opening for Divine intervention.

Life's Messages: As you create your affirmations, leave an opening for Divine presence. Know that infinite hope can shine light on the darkest of days. Allow hope to be your blanket of peace.

Chapter 12

Through The Eyes of a Child

And a woman who held a babe against her bosom said, "Speak
to us of Children."
And he said:
Your children are not your children.
They are the sons and daughters of Life's longing for itself.
They come through you but not from you,
And though they are with you, yet they belong not to you.
You may give them your love but not your thoughts.
For they have their own thoughts.
You may house their bodies but not their souls,
For their souls dwell in the house of tomorrow, which you
cannot visit, not even in your dreams.
You may strive to be like them, but seek not to make them like
you.
For life goes not backward nor tarries with yesterday.
You are the bows from which your children as living arrows are
sent forth.
The archer sees the mark upon the path of the infinite, and He
bends you with His might that His arrows may go swift and far.
Let your bending in the archer's hand be for gladness;

For even as he loves the arrow that flies, so He loves also the
bow that is stable.
-Khalil Gibran

"The Prophet" by Khalil Gibran is one of the books that allowed
me to embrace being on bed rest during my pregnancy with
Jackson. While I found this reading to be particularly poignant,
I did not immediately connect with the phrase "you may house
their bodies, but not their souls." It was not until after this
pregnancy ended that I came to understand the true meaning
of these words—that I gave this child physical form for a short
time, but that his soul was created by the same source that created
me—though the body is now an empty vessel, his soul continues
to live on.

It occurred to me that Jackson had received exactly what he
needed from me without being born into this world. He knew my
unconditional love when I surrendered to the fact that I would not
be able to carry his body to term and I was ready to accept him
however God intended him to be. All along I had been praying
for him to be born healthy. It was not until the eve of his birth
that I realized that good health was not a condition for my love. I
am grateful for having said the words, "I will accept you however
God wants to give you to me." I now see that my prayers did not
go unanswered—that he was born safely into the arms of God
and he will forever be a part of Life and a part of me.

In recent weeks, I have been noticing the numbers 1.1.1.0
wherever I look. I would look at a clock in my home, a cell phone
or the car and it would read 11:10. I would notice the numbers on
a license plate or in a store. I kept wondering what these numbers
meant. Then I just happened to look at Jackson's birth certificate.
I instantly made the connection. Jackson had been born on 1.1.10

at 11:10 pm. In that moment, I sensed that this was his way of letting me know he was nearby.

A Letter to Jackson

My dearest Jackson,

My love for you continues to live on. At times I do wish I could see you and touch you and watch you grow. That is the longing of a mother's heart—to cradle her infant child. I am only sad when I forget that you are still growing and evolving as all souls do. I am grateful that you chose me to give you life and love. I looked at your picture today and there were no tears. I just smiled. I never looked into your eyes, but I have felt the presence of your soul. While the sound of your heart beating has faded from my memory, your tiny footprints will forever remain in my heart. I love you. With eternal love, Mommy

As I finished this letter, I could feel a presence behind me. To attempt to put into words what I sensed, it was a shift in the air behind me. The air felt denser with warmth that made me tingle. Almost immediately, my yellow lab jumped up, scurried out of the room, but then stood outside the door and just looked in. This startled me. I have had similar experiences, but never before was it confirmed by another living being.

I was at a very different stage of my journey when Jade was born. In the losses I experienced prior to her, my grief was due to the disappointment of what could have been rather than a deep connection to a visiting soul. As with Reagan, I did not express my love for Jade in any way until she was in my arms. There had been no prenatal conversations. It was only as I held her close that I was capable of loving her completely. I knew right then that her life was not to be measured by how long her heart continued to beat.

The other visiting souls have taught me that love has no boundaries. Where there is a sense of connection, there is love. Where there is love, there will always be love. Yet, I have to let go of my idea that this love must exist in a physical, more tangible form.

I feel very blessed to have a surviving child. She is one of the greatest miracles in my life. I also have a deeper understanding of why we are meant to have this time together. She is clearly in my life to teach me as much I am to guide her in taking her place in this world. Even her un-explainable early entry and re-working of my birth plan helped me to be more accepting of *what is*. Three ultrasounds, including one on the day of her birth and I still had to wait until she was here to find out she was a girl. Yes, she still teaches me patience. She reflects back all aspects of me, positive and negative. She has taught me how to love gratuitously and continues to be a source of many lessons. In her early months, I was so captivated by how she experienced the world, discovering all the newness that surrounded her. I wanted so much to be able to see the world through her eyes. And, every day I get glimpses of how she sees the world.

I recall one December morning when we were hoping for the first snowfall of the season, but it rained instead. In her eyes, the next best thing would be to see a rainbow. I explained, as best I could, that it was unlikely after looking at the forecast that did not include any sun that particular day. As I headed down a flight of stairs with my breakfast shake in hand, the cover popped off as I was shaking it. My shake spilled all over and drizzled down the wall. She was only four and yet exclaimed, "Look momma, a chocolate rainbow!" So this is the title of our special book, *The Chocolate Rainbow*. It's about being able to see the beauty in what first appears to be a huge mess. One of our favorite lines in this rhyming story is, "While colorful rainbows must have sunshine, all a chocolate rainbow needs is a COLORFUL mind. "

At the time of this writing, my daughter is seven. As loving and as gentle as I am with her, she constantly asks for confirmation of my love. At first, I questioned her about this. Her response was that she liked hearing me say that I loved her. But then, it struck me that she was reflecting back the question I had often asked. *Do you love me?* While I never verbalized it, it was a constant thought. Before I understood the circumstances of my early years, I often questioned my mother's love for me. I wondered why my biological father was not a part of my life and I secretly longed for his love. I also spent much of my life seeking approval and recognition from others. I excelled as a student because this is where I most earned the recognition that I sought.

I know that it is by God's grace that I have emerged a loving woman. By reflecting back this exact question I once asked, my daughter has given me the opportunity to check in with that deep inner voice that now responds, *yes I do love you.* I am the love that I was seeking. I also recognize the importance of reminding that little child that lives within me that she is deeply loved.

Another lesson came more recently when my daughter was cutting and pasting from a magazine as part of a homework assignment. At the same time, she was singing a song, making up the words as she went along. She really caught my attention as she sang the words, "I'm doing what I was born to do." I said, "What a beautiful song." Then I asked, "So what were you born to do?"

She thought for a few seconds, then looked at me and said, "To be a kid." I smiled. I had expected her to say that she was born to be an artist because I can already see her affinity to creative expression. But then, I realized the real beauty of her response.

Life's Messages: Learn from the children in your life. Allow them to help you find the essential aspects of who you were created to be. Teach them how to live a life connected to the heart of who they are. Along the way, recognize how important it is to be inventive, to play and to simply have fun.

Chapter 13

Ever After

A dear friend shared a story about her mother's first experience upon arriving at a nursing home. She was then 92 and in a wheelchair. Her care plan included regular physical therapy so that she "could walk again." When the staff proposed this plan, she said "No thanks, I've walked long enough."

What I love about this story is this woman's ability to sit firmly in what she believed was best for herself and most honoring of her body. It is often easy to allow others to decide what our next step in life should be. Many well-meaning persons have shared their opinions about my journey. Our difficulty was not in conceiving, but in my ability to carry to full term. Some have asked if we would ever consider adoption. We have not explored this option because it has not presented itself to us. Assisted Reproduction is not what I ever thought we would explore; yet, the timing of receiving this offer soon after prayer is what allowed us to consider this path.

We still get asked why we chose to have an only child and have often been told, "Your daughter is so beautiful—you guys need to have another one." These are obviously people who have no idea of our experience. I used to be very sensitive to these questions and comments, but now understand that people are curious by nature and are guided by their own experiences and those in their close circle. My need to explain fully has disappeared with healing. Now, I just smile or simply respond by saying, "That's the way it worked out. We're happy we have her."

My cousin and her six year old daughter continue to live with us. Over the past year, I have come to really know and love her little girl. Our daughters share a bedroom and often claim to be sisters. They are truly like siblings. In one minute they are bickering and in the next, they are laughing, hugging each other and defending one another. While this is not the family I envisioned, I am grateful for this current arrangement.

There was a time I insisted that I did not ask for a spiritual awakening, but the following journal entry suggests otherwise.

Journal entry dated June 7, 2008....................*At present, my journey involves finding the way to living my fullest potential as a wife, mother, healthcare provider and person wanting to experience a life of few regrets and genuine happiness. Not only do I want to define my BEING and discover my true self, but I also want to better understand how my childhood has defined and molded my thoughts and actions. I want to uncover the root of my fears, beliefs, and desires. I seek to dispel those fears, strengthen those beliefs and achieve that which I most desire. I aspire to be confident, true to myself and to live a life with purpose. I want a healthy balance of structure and spontaneity. I hope to be a positive role model for Reagan, my beautiful daughter and any future children.*

All I can say after re-reading this is that I have to be really careful about what I ask for.

Journal entry dated June 10, 2008....................*Today is Jade's birthday. She would have been two. Ever since her birth and death, I have sensed that I am being called to utilize my gift of writing—to create a book that will help others. I thought that I would find the concrete answer for preterm labor, achieve a full term pregnancy and spare other women the grief of losing a child. But, now I realize that sometimes there are no answers and that my answer may not be their answer.*

I am keenly aware that Life's mysterious nature has brought me back to a childhood dream of sharing my writing. There were many times I wished I could have gotten to this point without the pain and the heartache. But, it could not have happened any other way. It is the pain that has opened me to the process of connecting with my deepest self and setting free the life that is within me.

Growth Journal entry dated October 30, 2011.................
This life within me can no longer be contained. It feels very much like a bursting forth…like the force of exploding fireworks except that it has a softer sound and the light burns eternally. This life yearns to be free, yet it is not invasive. It is colorful, yet not boastful. It is powerful, yet with a gentleness of heart. This is new—being able to describe this life so clearly. I can now see this life within me as being truly infinite and eternal…a beautiful creation of a loving God. It can only evolve and be transformed. It is as they say, love never dies. It only lives. For me, this now feels completely true.

The process of putting a pen to paper is truly something that makes my heart sing. In my earliest journal, I once wrote that *I love to write stories, but I want a career in helping people. Maybe I'll be a doctor, a pediatrician or something of that sort.* The date of this entry was the Fourth of July, 1989. Then, on October 3rd, 1989, I wrote that *I am going to write a story unlike any story I've ever written. It's going to be a real book.* I have no recollection of what that story might have been. My younger self did not realize that I could help others through my writing—and that story I would write, it would be my own life story.

One of my favorite movies is Andy Tennant's film, *Ever After,* a spin on the Cinderella fairytale. Like many others, I love stories with happy endings and miraculous outcomes. Yet, I am most touched by the closing line of this movie when the narrator says,

"And while Cinderella and her prince did live happily ever after, the point gentlemen, is that they lived."

I have become ever so mindful of what it means to truly live—to be aware of the presence of God within me and in those around me. My well-being is not determined by circumstances or dependent upon the personalities of those I encounter. I embrace each day with gratitude and my intent is to be fully present to others. I choose to infuse ordinary acts with love and joy—dancing as I vacuum or sweep the floors and singing as I do the dishes.

In that deepest space of my heart, I know that Life loves me and that I am still free to co-create my world and become all that I was intended to be. I affirm that everything I need comes to me in perfect sequence and time. When the time is right, we will move forward with the final embryo transfer. If another child is meant to accompany me on this journey, I trust that it will happen. Until then, I will do the best I can to accept what already is.

Life's Messages: Live the life you were created to live. See your life experiences as a treasure map, guiding you to unearth your unique gifts. Be a channel for love, joy and peace.

Afterword: Who Are You?

Who are you, really? When do you feel most like yourself? Your self-image and how others see you are often not the truest representations of who you are in your essence. There is a great deal of conditioning that begins from the moment of your birth. You can lose important aspects of yourself when love comes with conditions that you look and behave a certain way. Painful words or actions of others can shape your beliefs about yourself and the world that surrounds you. You are led further and further away from the person you were intended to be. You survive, but you are not whole. You present an appearance that hides great insecurity. You make choices that are not in line with what is most essential in you.

Still, at the HEART of who you are, lie your truest identity, your gifts and your truest purpose. There is an unyielding aspiration to express all of your inherent potential. Your BEING wants to thrive. This deep source of life wants you to recognize all of your aptitudes. It beckons you to give your full measure. There is often an unsettled feeling or sense of dissatisfaction that whispers to you. When ignored, these subtle whispers become resounding echoes. It is your heart's greatest desire that you return to the pure essence of who you really are.

How do you begin to reclaim your truest self? You first create conditions that allow you to connect with your BEING.

You spend time in silence and with nature. You listen to music and read books that nourish your soul. You surround yourself with persons who are affirming and life-giving. You pay specific attention to all that you are feeling and allow yourself to feel every emotion. And then, you trust. You trust that every sensation is signaling something meaningful and leading you onto a path of discovering your truest purpose.

How will you know when you have found your life's purpose? You will feel it emanating from the depths of yourself. There will be a sense of "oneness" and "rightness" between who you are and what you are doing. You will have said good-bye to shame, regret and guilt. Fear will also begin to dissolve. You will have recognized your gifts and decide to respect your limitations. You will be creating and contributing to society. You will radiate love, joy and peace.

The PRH Method of Self-Discovery

The PRH method of self-discovery is based on the concept that it is "natural for human beings to want to become more."[1] It is intended for persons whose primary focus is to live their life more fully and utilize all their gifts with a deeper sense of purpose. It offers a decision-making process and methodical writing tools that allow persons to get in touch with their own inner wisdom. They begin to recognize the positive aspects of themselves and accept their limitations with humility. It empowers them to make decisions and appropriate changes that are in line with what is most essential at the core of who they are. This also allows them to live their relationships better and to take their place in making their contribution to society. You may wish to visit www.prh-usa.com or www.prh-international.com to find an educator or workshops in your area or to learn more about the history of PRH and its founder, Andre Rochais.

Reclaiming your True Essence

Certain conditions are needed in order to connect with the truest and most positive realities that are at the core of your identity.[2]

1. **"Life-giving" or "Soul-nourishing" Relationships:** These are relationships that awaken in you the desire to be fully authentic. These relationships allow you the freedom to express yourself fully.

2. **Self-Affirmation:** You adopt a healthy self-image and recognize your deep values such as love, justice, truth, your capabilities, qualities and gifts *"of heart, of action, of the intellect, etc."*[3] You learn how to live and act in faithfulness to your deep inner conscience. You live from the being, but take into account the whole person—your intellect, your emotions and your body[4]

3. **Taking Time to Connect to Being:** The Being is a place of inner wisdom. It is that non-physical, pivotal center that holds your truest identity and all of your gifts. We *"instinctively"* seek to realize our truest purpose that has been inscribed within the being. This fundamental center also holds a dimension that bonds you to others in your sense of community as well as your spiritual dimension.

Four Steps to Awakening the "Being"

Step One: Silence the mind through a meditative practice or spending time alone in nature.

In PRH, this is specifically called "Time for being." It is when you allow yourself to just "be" and observe whatever arises in your best self. It has been described as "bathing in the positive aspects of ourselves so that we may feel young again, bringing back the original freshness and the gentle strength of being." It enlivens us so that we may "get ourselves going again in daily life, with new energy" and be able to carry out our commitments. It serves to help renew and build healthy relationships.[6]

If you struggle with most common forms of meditation, the practice of Qigong can be very helpful. It is a moving meditation and self-healing exercise that includes healing posture, self-massage, breathing techniques, combined with slow movement and silencing of the mind. There are techniques that are suitable for every age and physical condition.[7]

Step Two: Spend time writing about the "alive" feelings awakened in your body during the Time for Being. Keep a growth journal. Focus on yourself, not others. There is no blame, no judgment. Write with the intention of discovering or experiencing something new...a new aspect of yourself, more clarity, a freeing, anything that allows you to live your life better. PRH educators offer a methodical training to get you started on this type of journaling.

Writing helps you explore all of what you are experiencing. *What is this uneasiness linked to? Where is this self-doubt originating? Why is my heart racing? What is this deep sadness?*

It creates that space for your inner wisdom to speak. It can help you determine the true origin of what you are feeling. It can awaken essential aspects of your self. It takes time and much practice, but you are worth it.

Step Three: Be involved in a group and/or find someone who is a great listener and able to receive your story without judgment. Sharing your written work is essential. You will need a safe place, based on mutual respect and trust to continue on your growth journey. It provides an opportunity to talk about your lived experience. It allows others to see the REAL you, to witness your strengths, as well as your limitations and your weaknesses that you often try to conceal. Sharing and listening to others enable sensations to grow further and bring about new insights and other forms of awareness. Share your written work, honoring yourself and your writing. You share only when you are ready to and what you choose to. You use the pronoun "I" as opposed to "you" or "we" as to own what you are saying. You grow in truth and humility.[8]

Step Four: Spend time reading for the purpose of stimulating further insights and discoveries. In PRH, there are certain commentaries known as "Observation Notes." These are based on over four decades of research and observations of the human person and the mechanisms of growth. They are typically distributed to workshop participants after the sharing of their personal experiences.[9] They are essentially a compilation of the work of those who have walked this path of self discovery before you.

Nature Exercise

Go out into nature. Allow yourself to be drawn to an object, a tree, a rock or any other element that seems to "speak" to you. Be gentle with yourself as not to force anything. If you do not feel attracted to anything, just stay with the silence and see what arises from within you.

Walk, sit on the ground or do whatever feels comfortable and allows you to go inward and closer to yourself. Spend as much time as you are able to or feel that you need.

Allow your eyes to focus downward which reminds you to go into your heart or your core and not your head.

Then, take the time to journal about the sensations or feelings that were awakened during this time. It is important to remember that a sensation is not an idea or a memory, it is a feeling.

This exercise is best when done regularly.

During the learning stages, you may want to speak to a PRH Educator about your experiences with this method and to share your writing.

Questions for Exploration

We often need others to ask questions we don't think to ask of ourselves. Questions are important in facilitating an individual's search for in-depth understanding of oneself. The right questions can open pathways of exploration that allow you to live a more harmonious and fulfilled life.

Here are some questions to begin your trails of self-exploration. Always sign and date your work in your growth journal. This is your journey.

- Which aspects of my personality do I experience as positive? What gifts or talents do I possess? Where do my difficulties lie? If it interests me, I classify them, as follows: intellectual, manual, relating to action, artistic, relational, physical or others...
- Do I feel that I see myself in a balanced way? Do I see myself in mainly a positive or negative way?
- I observe a person I love or who has been a positive influence in my life. I describe what this person

awakens deep within me. What does this tell me about my own qualities?

- I observe the elements of my external environment that I like or that affects me positively (nature, music, arts, etc.) I describe what these elements awaken deep within me. What does this tell me about my own qualities?
- What in me has helped me to live through a difficulty or challenging situation in my life? In what ways have I grown or become stronger?
- What are my deep aspirations that I have not yet lived?

PRH Resources

[1]Observation Note "Times for Being" p. 2, 2005

[2]Persons and their Growth, the Anthropological and Psychological Foundations of PRH Education, p. 56, Poiters- France, 1997

[3]Observation Note "Diagram of the Pivotal Centers of the Human Person" p. 3, 2005

[4]Observation Note "General Introduction to PRH Education" p. 2, 2005
Note: Observation Notes are available to all participants of the workshop entitled, *Who Am I?*

[5]Persons and their Growth pp. 55-62, the Anthropological and Psychological Foundations of PRH Education, p. 56, Poiters- France, 1997

[6]Observation Note "Times for Being" p. 2, 2005

[7]The Way of Qigong, Kenneth S. Cohen, Ballantine Books-New York, 1997

[8]Observation Note "Sharing on GPA'S" p. 2, 2005

[9]Observation Note "General Education to PRH Education" p. 3, 2005

CPSIA information can be obtained at www.ICGtesting.com
Printed in the USA
BVOW072259220212

283593BV00001B/1/P